More Praise for *Teaching That Changes Lives*

"Marilee Adams is an engaging writer. Using the medium of story-telling, she clearly explains the importance of developing a Learner mindset and the necessity for educators to create inquiry-based learning environments infused with curiosity, creativity, and caring. Any educator in higher education and K–12 is sure to benefit from reading this valuable and practical book."

—**Patrick Blessinger, founder and Executive Director, International Higher Education Teaching and Learning Association**

"Offers a methodology for compassion…honors the power of the question and provides a gentle guide to a better kind of leadership. Great message. Very readable with tools and ideas that are easy to hold on to."

—**Peter Block, bestselling author of *Stewardship* and *Community***

"Dr. Adams has created a fundamental framework that's sure to lead educators, administrators, and students toward increased collaboration, problem solving, and greater success. This book is a must-read for anyone who cares about education and cares about the future. That means just about all of us."

—**Naomi Drew, educational consultant and author of *No Kidding about Bullying***

"Every teacher can find himself or herself in this story. We all have days when self-doubt or frustration threatens to overtake our passion and commitment for teaching. *Teaching That Changes Lives* reveals the power of every teacher's mindset to create a classroom climate that opens children's minds, helping every student become engaged with and love deep learning. This is a must-read for everyone who touches the curious minds of children—a message that has powerful implications for changing schools and changing lives."

—**Victoria Duff, President, Learning Forward New Jersey, and Senior Consultant, Center for Results, Learning Forward**

"What a joy it was to read your book! You are sharing numerous underlying messages about hope, the power of asking positive questions, the importance of knowing one's students, learning styles, making mistakes and learning from them, and more. This exciting book will undoubtedly have a far-reaching and generative influence on teachers and students at all levels."

—**Jenny Edwards, PhD, Professor, School of Educational Leadership and Change, Fielding Graduate University**

"Marilee's work has changed the life of my campus."

—**Verna Fitzsimmons, PhD, CEO, Kansas State University Salina, and Dean, College of Technology and Aviation**

"Best education book ever! Leverage the power of *choice* to ignite a passion for learning and change lives. Not only will you energize yourself as you read Marilee's dynamic book, you will finally have the tools to enrich the lives of your students as you challenge them to claim their greatness."

—**Vicki Halsey, PhD, Vice President, The Ken Blanchard Companies, and author of *Brilliance by Design***

"We have seen over and again that our mindsets impact all aspects of our work, forming the very foundation of trust, growth, and collaboration essential for achieving a positive staff culture, strong school culture, and, ultimately, academic success with our scholars. This book gives individuals at all school levels the tools necessary for building positive Learner mindsets…provides the 'missing link' in how to have a strong staff culture."

—**Camilla Lopez, Principal, and Kevin Lohela, Academic Dean, Achievement First Crown Heights Elementary School**

"This beautiful narrative, evoking the struggles and victories of real people and real situations, awakens our hopes and aspirations for igniting the love of learning, not just for our students but within the very heart of our own teaching…as useful for youth workers, camp counselors, and parents as it is for classroom teachers."

—**John McAuley, President and CEO, The Leadership Studio at Muskoka Woods, Canada**

"This book is a beautiful and compelling illustration of the power of positive psychology and resilience theory in education!"
—**Caroline Adams Miller, Master of Applied Positive Psychology and bestselling coauthor of *Creating Your Best Life***

"This is truly an inspiring story of learning and change. I love that change and learning did not happen just to students but to teachers as well...illustrates the impact of emotional intelligence in action... The transformative process embedded in the storyline is deeply beneficial and enlightening."
—**Kenneth Rhee, PhD, Associate Professor and Director, Executive Leadership and Organizational Change Program, Northern Kentucky University**

"If every teacher in America read this book, I believe it would have an incredible impact on student learning. Dr. Adams helps the reader identify and manage two powerful mindsets that live behind all our actions—the Judger and the Learner. If you are looking for a clear path for improving the learning of your students through your professional learning communities, this book will be indispensable for making that happen!"
—**James L. Roussin, coauthor of *Guiding Professional Learning Communities* and *Implementing Change through Learning***

"*Teaching That Changes Lives* kick-starts the learning journey for teachers, students, and school communities. Appreciative Inquiry in education is a perfect fit with the insightful questions and choices presented in this highly readable, usable book. Dr. Adams has made a major contribution to the strengths-focused education community."
—**Marge Schiller, PhD, founder, Positive Change Core, and coauthor of *Appreciative Leaders***

"An uplifting book with meaningful, appreciative strategies for teachers committed to making a positive difference in their students' lives...a genuine contribution to teachers and learners in any setting."
—**Jacqueline M. Stavros, DM, Professor, Lawrence Technological University, and coauthor of *The Appreciative Inquiry Handbook***

"*Teaching That Changes Lives* reminds us that at the heart of all good education are inquiry and a Learner mindset. This engaging and thoughtful book is filled with examples and simple, practical tools for creating a climate of learning where we can challenge our assumptions and change the questions we ask ourselves to build the education system of the future."

— **Kathy Telban, MEd, CPT, SPHR, Director of Curriculum and Assessment, Cuyahoga Community College, Cleveland, Ohio**

"*Teaching That Changes Lives* wisely reminds us that authentic teaching requires that we must model the behavior we teach or we cannot hope to influence the behavior—or the future—of our students."

— **Robert M. Tobias, JD, Director, Key Executive Leadership Programs, American University**

"This book re-ignites the raison d'etre for teaching—to change lives. Marilee gives teachers powerful and simple methods for getting on track for what *real teaching* and *real learning* are all about."

— **Dr. Henry Toi, founder and CEO, Nurture Craft Education Group, Singapore, and Publisher, *Brain Capital Magazine***

TEACHING
THAT
CHANGES
LIVES

TEACHING THAT CHANGES LIVES

12 Mindset Tools for Igniting the Love of Learning

Marilee Adams, PhD

BK

Berrett–Koehler Publishers, Inc.
San Francisco
a BK Life book

Berrett-Koehler Publishers, Inc.
235 Montgomery Street, Suite 650
San Francisco, CA 94104-2916
Tel: (415) 288-0260   Fax: (415) 362-2512   www.bkconnection.com

Ordering Information

Quantity sales. Special discounts are available on quantity purchases by corporations, associations, and others. For details, contact the "Special Sales Department" at the Berrett-Koehler address above.

Individual sales. Berrett-Koehler publications are available through most bookstores. They can also be ordered directly from Berrett-Koehler: Tel: (800) 929-2929; Fax: (802) 864-7626; www.bkconnection.com

Orders for college textbook/course adoption use. Please contact Berrett-Koehler: Tel: (800) 929-2929; Fax: (802) 864-7626.

Orders by U.S. trade bookstores and wholesalers. Please contact Ingram Publisher Services, Tel: (800) 509-4887; Fax: (800) 838-1149; E-mail: customer.service@ingrampublisherservices.com; or visit www.ingrampublisherservices.com/Ordering for details about electronic ordering.

Berrett-Koehler and the BK logo are registered trademarks of Berrett-Koehler Publishers, Inc.

Printed in the United States of America

Berrett-Koehler books are printed on long-lasting acid-free paper. When it is available, we choose paper that has been manufactured by environmentally responsible processes. These may include using trees grown in sustainable forests, incorporating recycled paper, minimizing chlorine in bleaching, or recycling the energy produced at the paper mill.

Library of Congress Cataloging-in-Publication Data
Adams, Marilee.
Teaching that changes lives : 12 mindset tools for igniting the love of learning / Marilee Adams, Ph.D. ; [foreword by] Arthur L. Costa, Bena Kallick.—First edition.
    pages cm
ISBN 978-1-60994-569-5 (pbk.)
1. Thought and thinking—Study and teaching—United States. 2. Cognition in children. 3. Effective teaching—United States. 4. Educational change—United States. I. Title.
LB1590.3.A34 2013
370.15'2—dc23
                                        2013021037
First Edition
18 17 16 15 14 13   10 9 8 7 6 5 4 3 2 1

Cover design: Irene Morris Design
Text design: Detta Penna
Proofreader: Katherine Lee

DEDICATION

*With respect and gratitude
for Dr. Bill Friedman and
every teacher who believes
that teaching changes lives*

CONTENTS

FOREWORD

We have devoted many years as educators to writing and teaching about the Habits of Mind—dispositions needed for productive thinking and problem-solving. Although many people refer to these dispositions as "soft skills" because their measurement does not yield "hard data," we nonetheless believe that these are essential skills that students need in order to succeed in the increasingly complex, uncertain future that awaits them. Happily, we are part of a large and growing community of educational authors, thought leaders, and teachers who share this belief and whose work is making a solid difference in many countries around the world. With *Teaching that Changes Lives*, Dr. Marilee Adams joins this constellation, contributing her insightful work on mindsets and questioning for the benefit and satisfaction of students and teachers alike.

Through the rich traditions of teaching through story-telling, Dr. Adams demonstrates how our mindsets—the perceptions we hold of the world—impact our students, our colleagues, and ourselves. In this engaging educational story, Marilee has captured key emotional and intellectual challenges that teachers encounter in today's classrooms, while weaving in practical, time-tested tools for meeting these challenges. The characters, drawn from real life, demonstrate how it is possible to literally *change the weather* in the classroom to gain optimal rapport, engagement, responsiveness, and learning.

The concept so artfully presented here is how a teacher's mindset, cognitive processes, beliefs, and mental models affect their behaviors and their ability to connect with their students.

Through the story we become aware of how our external, observable human behaviors are a result of our inner thoughts, decisions, and perceptions. The author leads us to the practical consideration of how a teacher can manage his or her mindset even in challenging circumstances.

Teaching that Changes Lives offers insights and tools to help teachers recognize and choose their own mindsets, building consciousness and skills for leading their classrooms and enhancing their students' learning. This mindset work holds real promise for contributing to the intellectual and emotional development of students. At the end of the book, Dr. Adams has included a comprehensive workbook with 12 practical, easy to apply tools for thinking about our own thinking and gaining new awareness of options and interventions that are congruent with our intentions. This material is an invaluable contribution to the body of work available for professional development for educators.

The implications of this work are not just for educators, however, but are for all of us to become more metacognitive in life—becoming more aware and skillful with our choices and decision-making processes, and more mindful of our actions and their effects on others, both in our schools and in our lives in general. *Teaching that Changes Lives* is a valuable contribution to our field. And it is an important reminder of the cognitive and collaborative skills required for encouraging more thoughtful students, classrooms and schools—as well as for building the next generations of thoughtful leaders who believe in their power to change themselves and thereby change the world.

Arthur L. Costa, Ed.D., Granite Bay, CA
Bena Kallick, Ph.D., Westport, CT
Co-authors, *Learning and Leading with Habits of Mind:*
16 Characteristics of Success
Co-founders, The International Institute for Habits of Mind

MINDSETS FOR LEARNING

The hidden curriculum . . . is the teacher's own integrity and lived conviction . . . It is the message which is written in a teacher's eyes throughout the course of his or her career. It is the lesson which endures a lifetime.

Jonathan Kozol

You wouldn't be reading this book today had it not been for the teacher who changed my life. As a youngster I was never a star student, though I always had a book in hand, often reading at night with a flashlight under the covers or hiding in the closet to finish a story long after my parents thought I was asleep. While I loved to read, school was often a struggle for me and I had little confidence in my own abilities. It was in graduate school that a single teacher, Dr. Bill Friedman, provided that magical combination of caring, connection, and intellectual conscientiousness wherein I was able to flourish. While Bill was demanding, he was also kind and patient, always letting me know he believed I could live up to the high standards he set for me. Over the years he helped me hone my natural curiosity into the kind of

1

disciplined question asking that is the foundation of critical and creative thinking—and thereby contributed to the path that has become my life's work.

Through Bill's tutelage I made some of the most significant changes of my life—in my mindset and in the beliefs I held about myself as a learner, thinker, and as a person. The evidence for those changes showed up in sometimes unexpected ways. Once, when another professor deeply critiqued one of my papers, I surprised myself by easily responding, "Okay. What do I need to learn to fix it?" If, instead, my old mindset had been in charge, I would have drowned in a familiar downward spiral of self-reprisal. Of course, that would have prevented me from learning from that professor and going on eventually to turn in an excellent paper. Now I remember that incident fondly as my matriculation into "mindset school," where we are all perennial students.

Almost everyone agrees that the overarching purpose of education is to prepare students for the future, yet never before has the future been more difficult to predict or prepare for. To borrow Neil Postman's metaphor, students who "enter school as question marks and leave as periods" will certainly be ill-prepared to face the uncertainty of a future where there are no easy answers. Consequently, being a teacher today is more challenging and potentially more exciting than ever before. The key is helping students develop excellent thinking skills[1] and the capacity to engage in vigorous problem-solving to tackle the novel situations that the future has yet to reveal. While it is essential that we teach the core skills of literacy, numeracy, and technology, students will need to be more curious and creative than ever before. They will need to be resilient and have effective skills for interacting and collaborating with others in positive and constructive ways.

This is why our schools and classrooms must provide environments that encourage students to develop a lifelong love of learning. These proficiencies are so important to businesses and organizations that many emphasize "continuous improvement," providing training focused on communication, decision-making, critical and creative thinking, building collaborative relationships, and general people skills.

Teaching interpersonal communication and thinking competencies is of a different order than teaching the ABCs or math, where "correct" answers are more easily tested. Even when students get all the right answers on subject area tests, it is no guarantee of their preparedness to pass the tests of life. Most of us recognize that answers typically *close* thinking while questions typically *open* it. Lest we forget, answers are only the *end point* of a process—they can be only as useful as the questions and thinking that *precede* them. In *Learning and Leading with Habits of Mind*, Doctors Arthur Costa and Bena Kallick write that we must be " . . . interested in not only how many answers students know, but also how students behave when they don't know an answer. We are interested in observing how students produce knowledge, rather than how they merely reproduce it. A critical attribute of intelligent human beings is not only having information but also knowing how to act on it."[2]

As fundamental as questions are for attaining knowledge and living our lives, it is easy to overlook the importance of the mindset from which a question is launched. One's mindset will have a huge impact on any answers or results that might follow. In the words of Stanford University researcher Carol S. Dweck, "When you enter a mindset you enter a new world."[3] She cites compelling evidence for the impact of mindset in multiple areas, especially in learning and intelligence, and discusses how mindset interventions can even help resolve conflicts between longstanding adversaries.[4]

Dr. Dweck's formidable research on the distinctions between what she calls the "growth mindset" and the "fixed mindset" is conceptually aligned with the Learner and Judger mindsets described in this book and in my two previous books, *The Art of the Question: A Guide to Short-Term Question-Centered Therapy*[5] and *Change Your Questions, Change Your Life: 10 Powerful Tools for Life and Work*.[6] An international bestseller, *Change Your Questions* was originally intended for a business and organizational audience but has acquired a wide readership among educators. These books illustrate how skillful "mindset management" can be strengthened through developing greater facility with the quantity and quality of the questions we ask ourselves and others.

Teaching that Changes Lives focuses first on the teacher's mindset and the impact of that mindset—Learner or Judger—on their students, and on their own satisfaction with the experience of teaching. As you read the pages ahead, you'll also see how these same skills increase teachers' job satisfaction, which according to reliable studies has hit the lowest point in a quarter of a century.[7]

The skills outlined in these pages help us stay calm and present in order to think clearly and strategically from moment to moment, including when leading a classroom. These skills also help us successfully manage difficult situations that are a part of everyday life in many classrooms. The focus is on cultivating the Learner mindset for professional development, enriching the climate of learning, whether it's with whole classrooms, individual students and colleagues, parents, or professional learning communities.

In writing *Teaching That Changes Lives*, I chose to employ the same allegorical form as I used with *Change Your Questions, Change Your Life*. According to the *Wikipedia*, allegory is "a device in which characters or events in a story, poem, or picture represent or symbolize ideas and concepts." Successful allegory takes us deeper into our own lives, empowering us with new thinking, skills, and possibilities. My readers often share how much they have personally benefited from the mixture of story and practical application that the allegorical form provides "lessons embedded in a page turner."

The narrator of the story is Emma Shepherd, a sixth grade teacher who is a composite of many people I have known and worked with. Hopefully you'll find the story of Emma's struggles, insights, and breakthroughs to be engaging and enjoyable to read, while keeping in mind that her character is a vehicle for illustrating the Learner Mindset System at the heart of this book. Another main character is Dr. Sophie Goodwin, a university professor in a school of education. Dr. Goodwin's early work developing the mindset system of tools had a powerful impact on Emma, when she had Sophie as her sixth grade teacher.

The mindset and questioning lessons woven throughout Emma's story are rendered into 12 practical, easy to apply tools presented in a workbook at the back of the book. Throughout the story there are instructive graphics, pull quotes, and tables that augment the text. At the end of the book there is also a link to free digital tools for reinforcing the lessons of the book.

Much of Emma's story takes place in her sixth grade classroom. I had very specific goals in choosing this grade as the setting for the story. First and foremost, this age group constitutes an important milestone, when students often develop their own intellectual interests and passions, sometimes independent of what they're being taught at school. Many educators and brain scientists believe that if we can deeply engage students in learning and thinking by sixth grade, we can not only keep them in school longer but encourage their continuing intellectual, social, and emotional development. Almost everyone understands that we need to find better ways of accomplishing this end. Dropout statistics indicate that a quarter of American students drop out of high school before graduation, and in urban areas those statistics are even more distressing.[8] Perhaps it's not surprising that teacher job satisfaction has also declined significantly.[9]

As I've mentioned, many educators have already read *Change Your Questions, Change Your Life*. If you are one of them, you'll find that these two books complement one another. While the settings, characters, and stories are different, both books focus on the importance of mindsets, thinking, and questioning to achieve desired results. *Teaching that Changes Lives* illustrates how the mindset tools that have proven so successful for readers of *Change Your Questions* can make a similar positive difference in the world of education. When teachers strengthen their ability to manage their own mindsets skillfully and intentionally, they become more effective and satisfied as educators. When students strengthen their ability to manage their own mindsets skillfully and intentionally, they become more effective and satisfied as learners.

Emma's story illustrates how she uses her newfound mindset skills to great benefit with her students and colleagues, and for herself personally.

It is my heartfelt desire that *Teaching that Changes Lives* might contribute to each reader's greater fulfillment and success as a teacher, educational leader, parent, or student. I can think of no better way to pay homage to my own teachers and what they contributed to my life. You can imagine how gratifying it was for me to find Bill—the teacher who helped change my life so long ago—and let him know I've dedicated this book to him!

CHAPTER 1

THE ALCHEMY OF INQUIRY

Not just part of us becomes a teacher.
It engages the whole self...
Sylvia Ashton-Warner

I leaned against the kitchen counter at our home on Cedar Avenue, gazing out the window into the backyard. Since it was during the Thanksgiving break at my school, our cherry tree was bare, the grass lifeless and brown. But inside, sunlight streamed through the stained glass artwork which hung in the kitchen window behind the sink, sending little rainbows of light all around the room. Tiny facets of color danced over my arms and apron. The real magic to me, however, glowed through the big question mark at the center of this artwork. Set in a simple wooden frame, a bit larger than a 3-ring binder, that colorful stained glass image was a poignant reminder of Sophie Goodwin, who had been my teacher in the sixth grade, a year that dramatically changed my life. Much later, when I myself began teaching, Sophie became the most important mentor I could ever have wished for.

At the bottom of the frame was a small silver plaque that Sophie had had inscribed years before. She said this quote had been a guiding principle throughout her life:

> The important thing is to not stop questioning.
>
> *Albert Einstein*

Why that quote was so important to her was a mystery at first. As a child, I couldn't have begun to imagine the essential relationship between Einstein's words and what Sophie would teach me about questioning, mindsets, thinking, learning, and listening. What I did know for certain was that Sophie had a miraculous ability to create a safe, open, and inviting climate for learning. She connected with her students in ways that awakened our minds so that we became more engaged and successful learners. I had experienced something in Sophie's very being, that is, in who she was when she walked into the classroom, that changed how I thought about myself and how I felt and thought about the world.

Many people said her abilities were a gift one is born with, the way some people say that a gifted artist's or musician's or scientist's gifts are innate and not something one can learn. However, Sophie would clearly show that her gift and her impact on students *could* be learned. After retiring from classroom teaching, she earned her doctorate, became a professor in a school of education and began mentoring other teachers, teaching them the tools she had developed over her lifetime as an educator. Veteran teachers, those just entering the profession, administrators, and educational leaders were soon finding their way to her classes.

As important as she'd been for me in the sixth grade, I had lost touch with Sophie until my second year of teaching, when

I was facing a crisis in my profession, and was on the verge of quitting. As a child, Sophie's influence changed how I thought about myself and my capacities as a student. Now, as an adult and a teacher, her wisdom helped me avoid what would have been one of the most disastrous decisions of my life. Only as an adult would I learn from her how to *apply* her wisdom and tools in an intentional and systematic way. And I believe I changed the person I am whenever I walk into a classroom. That's what this story is about. But more than that, this book is my way of honoring Sophie's dream of making her innovative and practical teachings widely available and easily accessible to others.

Sophie's work is not part of any formal curriculum you might run across. But I believe it is fundamental to helping teachers manage the incredible pressures they experience while also reaching their most gifted students as well as those who are struggling. Today, thanks to Sophie's methods, I am able to be the teacher I've always dreamed of being, leaving the classroom at the end of each day satisfied that I've made a valuable contribution.

This book has been a labor of love as I relived my experiences as Sophie's student and recorded what she later taught me about teaching when she became my mentor.

To give some background: Right after my graduate training, and eager to start teaching, I spent the whole summer job-hunting, but jobs were scarce for new teachers. I was on the verge of giving up and applying for a job at a coffee shop when a friend suggested I look into Greenfield Elementary, a school in transition, thanks to budget cuts and certain problems they were experiencing. There had been school closings in the district and several teachers had quit. The principal, Dr. Malstrom, who'd been there for years, had recently taken early retirement. Class sizes had been increased and non-academic programs dropped.

The school district was looking for teachers who would come in at the bottom of the scale, with minimal benefits. It didn't sound great, but at least I would be *teaching!* I'd figure out how to make it work for me.

On the plus side, the school had a new principal, Dr. Bob Marshall, who had already made a name for himself in education. I'd be co-teaching a combined fifth and sixth grade class with an experienced teacher's assistant, Mrs. Santiago. I accepted Greenfield's offer and my husband Jared and I rented a small house just a few miles from the school.

My first year at Greenfield went well enough, thanks to my own idealistic exuberance and Mrs. Santiago, who had four years of experience managing the classroom under the teacher I'd replaced. She had also been studying nights and summers to get her teaching certificate. I liked Mrs. Santiago, but felt she was clinging too much to methods she'd learned from Mrs. Peterson, and it seemed like she resisted almost any change I wanted to make. This became a growing source of conflict between us.

Like most schools in transition, morale had been low at Greenfield, though in the time he'd been there, Dr. Marshall had brought us a long way. He had secured additional funding, including a grant for a new computer lab, and we'd had a small increase in enrollment when a charter school merged their program with ours. Dr. Marshall's predecessor, Dr. Malstrom, had left behind more than a few wounds and antiquated policies that some of the staff didn't want changed. Dr. Marshall definitely had his work cut out for him. In spite of the progress he'd made, there were some teachers, Ms. Privet chief among them, who were still fighting to retain the old principal's methods and considered Dr. Marshall too *nice*. He seemed to take this resistance in stride, winning over his adversaries one by one, patiently, confidently, and with great skill. His plan was to build a collaborative learning community at Greenfield and he knew this couldn't happen by forcing people to immediately comply with new ideas and policies.

Mrs. Santiago and I had a combined class of 34 students, many of whom required more individual help than we had time for. I worried about the underachievers, of course. But I also worried whether our more eager students, even those who earned excellent grades, were learning how to *think*. As for discipline, we were still limping along with Dr. Malstrom's archaic point system that was posted on the bulletin board. The *best* kids got stars after their names; those who misbehaved got big Xs after their names and were threatened with calls to their parents, which most kids dreaded. Being a particularly regressive system, this chart was one of the few things Mrs. Santiago and I seemed to be in agreement on. We both wanted to change it. But there always seemed to be more pressing issues, so discussing it was put on hold.

In spite of it all, our class was doing okay. Our achievement scores were acceptable but this wasn't any great comfort to me. What bothered me most was what I was *not delivering* to our kids. By the middle of my second year of teaching, I was worn down by all my doubts, the burgeoning, distracting incidentals, and the extra duties I had to fulfill that had little to do with teaching. I felt overworked, stressed, and certainly underappreciated.

I often recalled how excited and engaged I'd felt in Mrs. Goodwin's class and longed to be able to create that same experience with my own students. Why did so many of our students seem unenthusiastic and disengaged? What was I missing? Education had to be more than what Mrs. Santiago and I were providing. Was it the kids—too much TV, too many hours playing electronic games, lack of parental guidance, a system gone awry? Regardless of the answers to those questions, I knew one thing for sure: what I experienced as a teacher fell short of what I'd dreamed was possible. I had never been so discouraged and disillusioned. There were days when a job at a coffee shop began to look pretty good to me.

One afternoon Jared picked me up after school. We'd made a date to shop for a new sofa, our first major purchase together if you didn't count the car we'd bought the year before. After that we had planned to treat ourselves to dinner at our favorite restaurant. But I wasn't feeling enthusiastic about anything. It had been a particularly frustrating day at school, culminating in an argument with Mrs. Santiago over practically nothing. I'd ended up apologizing but I was sure it was going to leave bad feelings.

Jared and I pulled into the parking lot at the mall and he shut off the engine of the car. Instead of getting out right away he reached over and lightly rested his hand on my shoulder.

"What's going on with you lately?" he asked. "You seem a million miles away."

I wanted to lean over, lay my head on his shoulder and have him assure me that everything was going to be okay. But I knew he couldn't fix what was wrong. I admit I can get a little edgy when I've reached my limits, and this was one of those days. I just wanted to go home, climb into bed, and pull the covers over my head.

"I'm wondering why I ever got into teaching," I blurted out. "It isn't turning out the way I expected. Not at all."

Jared looked shocked, and a bit irritated.

"But that's been your dream for as long as I've known you," he said. "Can't you talk to a supervisor or something? Maybe your principal? There have to be other teachers who could help you."

Truth be told, I desperately wanted to talk with other teachers, but it seemed like everyone had their own problems. And anyway, why would they care about me, a relative newcomer? If I told Dr. Marshall about my dissatisfactions, I was pretty sure he'd dismiss me on the spot, or at least start looking for someone to replace me. Sitting there in the car, I tried to tell Jared about what was bothering me and he did his best to understand. I had a long list of grievances. Mostly, however, I had questions: Why did I feel so dissatisfied and down on myself about being a teacher? Why didn't I feel excited about teaching? Why didn't I feel more connected with my students? And why couldn't I make things work better with Mrs. Santiago? Most of the time, I just felt annoyed and resentful toward her.

These thoughts and feelings plagued me even more than the escalating pressures of too much paperwork, too little time, and too little money in the budget for some of the things Mrs. Santiago and I wanted for the classroom. Not to mention the omnipresent awareness that both of us were technically *on probation*. Any day we could get the news that we wouldn't be hired back for the coming year. I had tried to remind myself to take it one day at a time, but that old adage was wearing thin.

Jared and I sat and talked for a long time, and he did his best to be helpful. The only thing that came out of it was the decision to put off buying a new sofa. Taking on another big expense when I was so unsettled about my job didn't make sense. We cancelled our dinner reservation and picked up a pizza on our way home. I felt terrible about spoiling the evening but couldn't pretend any longer that everything was okay.

My self-doubts gnawed at me more each day as I racked my brain for solutions. Maybe I just wasn't cut out for teaching after all. I couldn't go on the way things had been going. It finally came to a head late one Friday afternoon as I sat alone in my empty classroom. In the distance I heard the whine of the janitors' vacuums and the shouts of children out on the playground. I stared off into space, feeling like the dark cloud hovering over my head would be there forever. Where was the excitement about learning I'd experienced as a young student? Mrs. Goodwin had worked her magic on all of us when we were kids, but it was painfully obvious I didn't have her gifts or her patience. I wasn't as good as she was, and never would be.

What happened next certainly wasn't a plan on my part but a reaction to the dissatisfaction and frustration I'd felt building up in me. As I was leaving school I noticed that Dr. Marshall's door was open and he was doing some paperwork. He looked up as I knocked lightly and apologized for disturbing him. He smiled and gestured to a chair across from his desk, inviting me to sit down.

I knew I needed to say what I had to before I changed my mind or lost my courage. Once I got started, the words came out in a rush. "I thought I should tell you that I'm seriously considering leaving teaching. I'll finish out the year but if someone comes along to replace me, I'll step aside."

As these words left my lips I felt a big knot twisting in my stomach.

"Every Monday morning when I walk into school," I continued, focusing my eyes on a light-colored rectangle where a picture had once hung on the wall behind Dr. Marshall, "I just feel hollow. I know it's because I'm not delivering what these kids deserve and what they need. Isn't that proof that this isn't where I belong?"

When I turned my attention back to Dr. Marshall's face, I was startled to discover that he was actually smiling, not unkindly, but as if he just had some brilliant insight.

"Emma," he said, "this may sound crazy to you right now, but I believe your misgivings say something positive about you. I hear your concerns, and I've observed your teaching. I can tell how much you care about your students and about teaching. Believe me, I would never have renewed your contract if I hadn't been pretty sure of you." He paused, I guess to let his words sink in. Then he added, "Fortunately, I know someone who may be able to help you. I'm sure she'd be willing to speak with you if I ask her."

He told me that some years ago, he'd been at a similar life impasse. He'd almost left education until he learned about the importance of mindsets and asking new questions that transformed what he thought was possible. He said that some kind of alchemy happens when we change the questions we ask ourselves. My face must have expressed bewilderment because he chuckled and added, "You'll find out what I mean soon enough." He didn't go into details, but tapped a few keys on his keyboard, then jotted something on the back of one of his own cards for me.

"I'm sure you'll like this woman very much. Please speak with her before you make a decision. She's semi-retired but teaches at the university and still mentors a few teachers. I'll give her a call and let her know you'll be contacting her. After you've met with her, let's get together and discuss your next steps."

I took the card and nodded, wondering what I had gotten myself into. I thanked him, went out to the parking lot, and climbed into my car.

I slumped behind the wheel and wondered if I had made a big mistake by talking with Dr. Marshall. Had he been nice to me, bolstering my morale, only because he didn't want to bother looking for another teacher? Would admitting my shortcomings hurt my record? No matter. What's done was done. I glanced down at his card, stared at his name for a second and then turned the card over.

This had to be a mistake! The name he'd written on the card was Dr. Sophie Goodwin. Could this be *my* Sophie Goodwin, my sixth grade teacher? That would be too much of a coincidence.

Driving home that afternoon, I kept seeing Mrs. Goodwin's face in my mind's eye and remembering moments from her classroom. What a wonderful year that had been in my life. I'd been this plugging-along kid before that, making do and just getting by. During her class I came alive to the experience of thinking and learning, even enjoying working on projects with other students. Mrs. Goodwin had been the first person to plant ideas in my mind of going into teaching someday. Who am I kidding? She was practically the first person to recognize that I even existed. At least that was how it felt at the time.

At home, I did a computer search for the university where Mrs. Goodwin taught, then clicked through to the faculty bios. My heart skipped a beat as Mrs. Goodwin's picture came up on my screen. Though she looked older than the idea of her in my mind, there was no mistaking that smile. It really *was* her. And she really had become *Doctor* Sophie Goodwin!

I started to dash off an email to the address listed with her bio. Then I thought better of it and decided on a handwritten note. The next day I bought a card with a beautiful nature scene and wrote her a message, including my email address and information about myself, such as when I'd been her student, and how Dr. Marshall had suggested I meet with her. After mailing the card, I felt hopeful for the first time in weeks. If anyone could help me, it would be Mrs. Goodwin.

It seemed like an eternity passed with no reply. Had Dr. Marshall told her something about me that put her off? I could hardly imagine Mrs. Goodwin not responding right away. Poor Jared had to listen to all my anxieties as I waited for her reply.

Then one morning an email from Mrs. Goodwin popped up on my screen. "I would love to meet with you," she said. She apologized for what she called her "tardiness." Personal matters had come up. She didn't give any details.

To my surprise she suggested that we meet the following Saturday at her place, about an hour's drive from my home. We'd have tea and talk things over, she'd said.

The morning of our meeting, I phoned to confirm the time. During the call I addressed her as Mrs. Goodwin, as was my habit. Embarrassed, I corrected myself: "I suppose I should call you *Doctor* Goodwin now."

She quickly corrected me: "Oh, for goodness sake, Emma, please call me Sophie. You don't need to be so formal, and besides, we're not in school anymore."

To a stranger's ears, those words might have meant very little. But for me they had a comforting inference. This was my hero, the teacher who'd changed my life. More to the point, her upbeat, optimistic tone made me feel better than I had in a long time. Maybe it was possible for me to pick up some of her teaching techniques. But maybe she'd simply help me clarify why I should change careers.

My answer would come over tea.

CHAPTER 2

MINDSETS MAKE ALL THE DIFFERENCE

Seek opportunities to show you care.
Kids don't remember what you try to teach them.
They remember what you are.
Jim Henson (Creator of The Muppets)

On Saturday, my GPS led me to Sophie's address at Hillview Apartments, an attractive building with large windows that let in plenty of light. It was surrounded by well-manicured lawns and beautifully tended flowerbeds.

I was buzzed in at the glass door in the vestibule and took the elevator to the third floor. As the door slid open, I found Sophie waiting for me in the hall. My heart skipped a beat. Her warm smile instantly reminded me of how *seen* and appreciated I had felt in her class. I had become the kind of student that had seemed impossible to me before that. Recalling all of this, I was nervous that she would be disappointed in me when she found out about my present problems. I was certain I hadn't lived up to her expectations.

Sophie gave me a brief hug which instantly put me at ease, just as her presence had made me feel more at ease in the sixth grade. I was startled by how frail she felt, reminding me of how much time had passed since I'd last seen her. But as she led me briskly down the hall to her apartment, she seemed as peppy and vital as ever. By the time we reached her door, she was excitedly sharing a story about the course she was teaching at the university, as if we were colleagues.

She gave me a quick tour of her apartment, explaining that she had moved here four years ago, soon after her husband died. It had been a difficult transition, she said, but she now felt quite connected to her new friends here.

Her expansive living room was furnished like a study, with floor-to-ceiling shelves along two walls, holding everything from children's books to the classics, as well as books on education and philosophy.

A large, high-definition computer monitor sat on a massive mahogany library table that I was sure must have an interesting history. Next to the computer keyboard were some leather-bound journals and stacks of paper that looked like a manuscript in progress. Was Sophie writing a book?

I turned my attention back to the screensaver on her computer monitor, which had aroused my curiosity the moment I saw it. It was some kind of map: *The Choice Map*, it said at the top of the screen.

"Does any of that look familiar?" Sophie asked, noticing my interest in the map.

"The Learner and Judger paths," I puzzled. "I remember something about them. But not the map, though I do have a vague memory of some sketchy lines you drew on the white board." As I studied the Choice Map, memories of her teachings about the Learner and Judger paths slowly made their way back into my mind.

There were two paths one could follow, each with distinctly different destinations. The Learner path led upwards to a beautiful bright sun. The Judger path led downward to a pool of mud. I couldn't help but notice a figure stuck in the mud who looked pretty miserable. That was how I'd been feeling lately—miserable and stuck in the mud.

I studied the figures on the different paths. They all had thought bubbles over their heads with questions that I quickly saw were very different, depending on which path they were on, the Learner mindset path or the Judger mindset one. I knew what mindsets were, of course, but I had lots to learn about Learner or Judger ones.

As I puzzled over the map, I remembered something Dr. Marshall had said about learning to manage his mindset by asking new questions that transformed what he thought was possible. Would this map help to explain what he was talking about?

"Make yourself comfortable while I get us some tea," Sophie said. She disappeared into the next room while I settled into a comfortable chair from which I could view the Choice Map. Sophie returned with a tray that held a beautiful hand-painted tea service.

Over tea and Sophie's delicious home-baked blueberry muffins, I gave her the *Cliff Notes* version of my life since the sixth grade. This retelling led naturally to my difficulties at school. Sophie listened with rapt attention, interrupting now and then to ask questions.

As our conversation progressed, we turned our attention to her Choice Map. She described how she had continued developing it long after I was her student. She said she thought it could help me now with the difficulties I had described in my note.

"Each year of teaching helped me refine what I was discovering about mindsets and how to reach my students," she said.

Choice Map™

We choose moment by moment

- What assumptions am I making?
- What are the facts?

- What happened?
- What do I want – for both myself and others?
- What can I learn?

Choose

Learner Mindset

Judger Mindset

START

React

- Why am I such a failure?
- Why are they so stupid?
- Why bother?

To download a color version of the Choice Map and to see a video explanation of it: www.LearnerMindsetOnline.com

JUDGER PIT

"In the beginning, it was mostly intuitive and evolved from my observations about how children learn best. Today I use the Choice Map to demonstrate to my graduate students how our questions reflect our mental attitudes, that is, our *mindsets*, and how these mindsets can influence everything in our lives—how we think and feel and behave and interact with others. The term mindset represents the set of beliefs and assumptions we hold about ourselves, others, and the world. It's mindsets that make all the difference. The Choice Map illustrates a whole system of mindset tools that can be helpful for teachers and students alike.

"It comes down to this: when you walk into the classroom, your own mindset makes all the difference in the world. It affects how you connect or don't connect with each child, and in turn how they connect with you. That connection, of course, will influence what your students are able to take in. It affects what they feel is expected of them and how encouraged or discouraged they'll be about learning to use their own minds and thinking for themselves. Your mindset creates the *climate*, the *weather* in the classroom."

> The term mindset represents the set of beliefs and assumptions
> we hold about ourselves, others, and the world.

"The weather?" I asked. "I don't understand."

"I read something many years ago that struck a chord with me. I recited it to my students so many times that I've learned it by heart. The author was Haim Ginott, a teacher and child psychologist. He said, *'I've come to a frightening conclusion that I am the decisive element in the classroom. It's my personal approach that creates the climate. It's my daily mood that makes the weather ... In all situations, it is my response that decides whether a crisis will be escalated or de-escalated and a person humanized or de-humanized.*"[10]

"Are you kidding? It's *my* mood that makes the weather in the classroom? That's pretty daunting," I said.

"Yes, it can be," Sophie said. "But you'll discover it's also empowering. Another educator, Robert J. Marzano, makes the same point in a different way: *The relationship between the inner world of a teacher's thoughts and emotions and the outer world of a teacher's behavior has been recognized for years—in research on teacher expectations; teacher beliefs about collective efficacy; and teacher and student perceptions of self-efficacy.*"[11]

"That makes sense," I said. "But what can we do about it? It seems like our mindsets are constantly changing, depending on so many things, both inside and outside us."

Sophie pointed at the Choice Map. "Look at that figure standing at the crossroads on the left between the Learner and Judger paths. What are the words you see circling around its head?"

"'Anything that impacts us at any moment—thoughts, feelings, circumstances,'" I read. "Are you saying that these create the weather?"

"Exactly," Sophie said. "And therein lies the challenge. We can't control what happens to us but we do have choice about what we do next. The Choice Map provides a way of *managing how we respond to circumstances* and even our own thoughts and feelings. It shows ways to monitor and change our thoughts, feelings, and actions from moment to moment." Sophie touched the wireless keyboard in her lap and a cursor popped up on that figure standing at the junction between the two paths. "In responding to the weather, people will take one of those two paths: Learner or Judger. Those paths represent our mindsets. And to tell the truth, when we're upset or things don't go our way, our natural reaction is to head right down the

Judger path. You see, that's everybody's default position. We're all recovering Judgers."

We're all recovering Judgers.

"Back in sixth grade," I said, "you helped me become aware of the thoughts and feelings I was holding in my mind. I guess these were creating my weather—my inner weather! Most of the time I was a big storm inside, but I never thought about it. I just took it for granted that what I believed about myself was . . . well, just the way it was for everyone. I certainly never imagined I had any power to change anything."

"Tell me more," Sophie said.

Encouraged by her response I went on: "That year my brain began working in ways that were absolutely new to me. Before your class I always felt that maybe there was something wrong with me. I wasn't very bright. Maybe it was the usual kid stuff, you know, when you're just sure you're the only one in the world who doesn't have all the answers. I was always thinking things like: *Why am I always messing up? Why don't I know how to do this? Other kids don't have problems like this.* I know I acted pretty dull, too. But soon, thanks to you, I stopped going so Judger on myself. I really did change, didn't I?"

"You certainly did! Watching students change and grow, as you did, is a teacher's greatest reward. I kept track of you, you know. You eventually went on to win academic honors and, as I understand it, you did extremely well at college and in your graduate studies."

"You know all that about me?"

"Oh, sure," Sophie said. "I do like to keep up on my kids."

"I'm embarrassed to tell you what I mostly paid attention to in class," I said. "For example, I worried about how I could keep from being noticed, or what did I had to do to just get by? I wanted to be invisible so nobody would find out what a loser I was. But then something clicked for me. It started when I discovered that in your classroom it was safe to be *visible*. I didn't have to hide. I guess you'd say I learned about the Learner path. I started regaining that sense of curiosity and wonder I had when I was a little kid. I remember, too, that I started participating in class and finding I could actually contribute something. I wasn't afraid to ask questions anymore. You didn't just want us to remember things so we could get the right answers on a test. I found out what it meant to think my own thoughts and really *understand* what I was learning. It was exciting, really exciting."

I couldn't have explained all this when I was a child, of course, but I do remember feeling respected and valued for myself, for being *me*. That was a new experience in my life. Sophie brought that kind of respect to the classroom. Now I understand that this came from her *mindset*. I always knew she was really happy to be there with us. I felt like my own ideas, my questions, and my curiosity were important. Sophie had a way of making us each feel like we *mattered*. She cared about *us* and not just about our grades.

I thought I was going to tear up as I recalled these experiences, but I took a deep breath and continued. "You taught us that making mistakes didn't mean we were dumb; on the contrary, mistakes were usually opportunities for expanding our knowledge. I stopped getting mad at myself for messing up. I think that's when I first realized that being smart isn't just about memorizing from some books. It's about keeping my curiosity revved up and asking lots of questions and believing that I could actually learn."

"Yes," Sophie said enthusiastically. "When we're in Learner mindset we're in a curiosity-and-questioning mode. It's wonderful to hear how much you remember. You'd be surprised how quickly children forget what they've learned, especially when they get so focused on taking home a good report card. Well, of course, you do know that by now."

Learner mindset means being in a curiosity-and-questioning mode.

We both laughed, though there was certainly a serious side to all of this.

"Everything you're saying tells me you're no stranger to the art of self-observation," Sophie said. "And this is so important, noticing, that is, observing what's going on in your own mind. It's the foundation of the system I teach in my grad course at the university. Being able to observe yourself is essential for anyone who wants to be able to monitor and manage their own mindsets. That level of self-awareness is at the heart of being a teacher who can make a real difference in students' lives."

Even as she said this, I plunged into Judger, picturing my students' faces as it struck me that their experiences were nothing like what I'd experienced in Sophie's sixth grade class. Not even close. My eyes stung like somebody had slapped me.

I thought about Becky, a girl I had tried very hard to reach. I winced as I recalled a disastrous meeting I'd had with her recently. She'd submitted a short writing assignment and, as I'd expected, most of her writing was sloppy and thoughtless. But there were four excellent sentences in the middle of her work, indicating that she was far more capable than I'd thought. I had been certain she always dashed off her assignments just to get through them. After reading those surprising sentences, I got excited about bringing out her true capabilities. She needed a pep talk. I don't remember my exact words to her but the gist was that she had *a lot of potential*. She could be getting As if she only learned to apply herself. When I told her that, Becky just stared at me blankly. Her face suddenly contorted and she burst into tears.

"Everybody's always telling me that," she had sobbed. "I don't know what you're talking about. I can't do it. And I hate school."

What was wrong with that child? She acted like I was punishing her and I was just trying to help. I tried to smooth things over, but she picked up her backpack and bolted from the room. Even worse, she was absent the next day and I blamed myself.

I also thought about Brandon. The way he acted out and put other kids down with his remarks really got under my skin. I knew I was critical and overly harsh with him. I was even making extra heavy Xs after his name on that Behavior Chart of Dr. Malstrom's, just to emphasize how angry he made me.

Not to mention my deteriorating relationship with Mrs. Santiago. How could I forget that?

"Are you okay?" Sophie asked.

"I hardly know where to start," I said, feeling myself getting wound up. "Mrs. Santiago, my co-teacher, is so rigid and set in her ways it makes me want to scream." As those words escaped from my lips, I immediately regretted them. Mrs. Santiago was a bright, well-educated woman who'd worked hard to get her teaching credentials. Maybe I was the stupid one. Why couldn't I figure out how to get through to her, or to my students, for that matter?

For a moment I felt as speechless as I'd first felt going into the sixth grade. I turned my attention back to the Choice Map and started reading the questions in the bubbles over the figures' heads. It took but an instant to see that the questions I was asking—about my students, Mrs. Santiago, and even myself—were all solidly on that Judger path.

CHAPTER 2 : Mindsets Make All the Difference

"I think I need a mindset adjustment," I mumbled, trying to make a joke of it.

Just then there was a knock at the front door.

"Please excuse me for a moment," Sophie said. "That would be my neighbor, Charlotte. She's an avid gardener. She oversees the neighborhood co-op garden down the street, and promised to bring me some flowers from their greenhouse."

I breathed a sigh of relief, grateful for the interruption. While Sophie went to answer the door, I retreated to the powder room. Once inside, I burst into tears. Gazing at my reflection in the bathroom mirror, the face that stared back at me seemed like a stranger's. I guess I hadn't been noticing the tension and frustration my face was expressing lately. I even looked a little hard, anything but receptive. Was this the face I presented to my students each day? Who was I when I walked in the classroom? What impact was my current mindset having on the kids? And what impact was it having on Mrs. Santiago?

Something I'd observed in Sophie, both when I was very young and in our meeting today, kept playing at the edge of my awareness. It had to do with the *quality* of her presence and how the room seemed to light up when she was there. Was this what she meant about *creating the weather*? I washed my face, touched up my makeup, and walked back into the living room as Sophie was saying goodbye to her neighbor Charlotte.

"This is one of the perks of having great neighbors," Sophie said, admiring the flowers she'd just received. "I'll put these in some water and be back in a second. Then let's talk a little about that mindset adjustment of yours."

CHAPTER 3

MAPPING THE GEOGRAPHY
OF OUR MINDS

When you enter a mindset, you enter a new world.

Carol S. Dweck

Sophie put the flowers into a large vase and brought them back to the living room. Their color and fragrance lifted my spirits.

"Are you okay?" she asked, turning to me.

"I'm actually fine," I assured her, knowing that my reddened eyes were sending a different message. "It isn't easy for me to look at how often I go Judger. Lately, I think it has completely taken over my internal climate. So please go on. What you're saying is all very helpful. I know I can't just be thinking about myself. I have to think about my kids, their grades, and their test scores—not to mention whether they're really learning, or accomplishing anything worthwhile."

"Oh, absolutely," Sophie said. She was silent for a moment. Then she asked quietly, "Do you think your students will learn more and as you said, *accomplish* more—in a Learner climate or a Judger one?"

31

The answer to that question seemed obvious but it also opened up a lot of other questions for me. After a moment I reflected, "It's painful to think of myself this way, I mean, as a Judger kind of person. I certainly don't want to be that way."

Do you think your students will learn more in a
Learner climate or a Judger one?

Sophie held up her index finger, gently signaling for my attention. "You bring up an important point," she said. "The Choice Map is *not* about labeling other people or putting them in boxes. And that certainly applies to ourselves. Nobody should be pigeonholed as a Judger or a Learner. Rather, the Choice Map is about recognizing the mindset we're in from moment to moment. Every single one of us has both Learner and Judger mindsets."

"That's reassuring," I said, trying to sound lighthearted. "I'm afraid I've been doing a big Judger number lately and putting a lot of people and circumstances into boxes. And, yes, that includes sticking myself in one of those boxes!"

"Just remember, having Judger moments is part of being human," Sophie said. "Our brains are hardwired like that. While there's no escaping this fact, understanding how it works is actually liberating. That's why I say we're all recovering Judgers. When you have a simple method for neutrally observing your thoughts, feelings, words, and actions, you vastly improve your choices about what to do next. We're talking about being able to respond effectively to whatever happens, instead of just automatically reacting. With the Choice Map and your observer self, you can choose your mindset. It always starts with your observer self."

"That's the art of self-observation you talked about," I said. "The image I get in my mind is being an explorer consulting a map to locate where I am."

"Yes," Sophie said. "Your observer self is the part of you that notices, 'oops, I just called that person the wrong name,' or 'oops, I've just taken a wrong turn.' It also helps us to identify whatever thoughts and feelings we're having without getting stuck in them. Real choice and control begin with having a strong observer self. The more you develop that inner capacity, the more you can see things in a neutral and open-minded way, like watching a movie of your life rather than just being in it. Sometimes, I tell myself, 'Okay, Sophie, it's time to quiet your mind and let your senses just take in what's really there, without projecting your own special meanings or taking any action. Just be mindful. Notice your mood, your thoughts, your feelings, and the circumstances that are impacting you, without adding layers of your own interpretation or judgments.'"

"Ah," I sighed, feeling more relaxed. "Life would be so much calmer and simpler if we could just stay in this observer self all the time. That would make it easier to stay out of Judger mindset, too."

Sophie chuckled. "I'm afraid we humans aren't built that way, unless you're a yogi living alone in a cave with minimal distractions. The rest of us live in a highly complex world, with things coming at us all the time from every direction. The point is that the more mindful we can be the better we can manage all those stresses and pressures.

"Being human, we're constantly shifting back and forth between Learner and Judger mindsets, hardly aware we're doing it. Nor do we realize that we have any control over choosing our mindsets, about which one is to be in charge. It's like either we have our mindsets or our mindsets have us. The Choice Map helps us expand our ability for observing our own thoughts, feelings, and questions, even our self-talk and how we communicate with other people."

"Including what we bring to our students," I said, thinking out loud.

"*Especially* what we bring to our students," Sophie said. "In the classroom having the ability to choose your mindset can make the difference between engaging your students or having them tune you out. And from your personal perspective, it can make the difference between your teaching experience being discouraging, boring, or even maddening; or being truly exciting and rewarding.

"At least most of the time," she added, and we both laughed.

"That's how I always dreamed it could be," I said, longingly. "Do you really think I can learn to do what you're describing?"

"I am completely confident you can. The art and *practice* of self-observation can be as simple as continually asking yourself: *Am I in Learner mindset or Judger mindset right now?* We all have the capacity to develop our observer self. It's part of our natural makeup, but as with learning anything new we need practice, and tools like the Choice Map really help. Just remember that mindset refers to the direction of our thinking, so you get to choose if you want to go in a Learner direction or a Judger one."

Am I in Learner mindset or Judger mindset right now?

"It's awfully easy to lose our way in the geography of our own minds," I reflected.

"Oh, that's wonderful," Sophie said. "Say that again."

"You mean *the geography of our minds?*"

"That's it," Sophie enthused. "My grad students will love

it. I'm going to steal that phrase from you. You don't mind, do you?"

"No, not at all."

Sophie clapped her hands. "Good! Good! The Choice Map helps us navigate through the geography of our own minds. You can see how each path on the map—Judger or Learner— leads into very different worlds. And because we create our own worlds, moment by moment, through our listening, our thinking, our speaking, and our actions, we can change the world we experience by changing how we think and speak, act, and listen. That's what change is all about. So the Choice Map is a guide for thoughtful change."

"Can you offer some simple examples?" I asked.

"Sure," Sophie replied. "When you're under pressure, people tend to go into survival mode, which manifests in a fight, flight, or freeze reaction.[12] Feelings like fear, anxiety, anger, or frustration can take over. Old issues bubble up in our minds, most of them having nothing to do with the present moment. To put it more poetically, we get *hijacked by Judger*. Our brains react like we're being stalked by the proverbial tiger that isn't actually there. Grrr, growl!"

A Judger hijack is like a fight, flight, or freeze reaction.

We both laughed at Sophie's tiger imitation.

"But if there really is a tiger, this reflex can be pretty useful," I said.

Sophie nodded. "Indeed! That's why developing our observer self is so critical. We need to be able to discern the true nature of any perceived threat, particularly with important people and relationships in our lives."

"Much less with those who are particularly irritating..."

I stopped myself in mid-sentence, pressing my hand to my mouth. I was thinking about school and Mrs. Santiago. She was a big problem. At least that's how I felt. Just seeing her at school every day raised my hackles. I went Judger big time. If only I could run the class exactly as I wanted, I'd be okay. Maybe this was too simplistic. Mrs. Santiago had her own issues with me, I guess. I sometimes thought she perceived me as that proverbial tiger after her, and I was anything but that. I was more like a leaf tossed around in the wind.

"Keep going," Sophie said. "You were about to tell me about people who are particularly irritating. This would be an excellent way to demonstrate how to apply the Choice Map in real life. Look again at the figure at the starting point of the Choice Map. It's a reminder that at any given moment of our lives, things happen. We may not have control of those circumstances or people, but we do have choice about what we think and do next and about which mindset we will step into and follow."

I guess I wasn't ready to talk about my problems with Mrs. Santiago and my own classroom. It was still a little too close to home. Besides, my eyes were drawn to that figure stuck in the mud at the end of the Judger path. I almost felt like I was traveling back in time, back to my childhood and Miss Hackett's fifth grade class. She talked to us like we were dummies, as though we didn't matter at all. Sometimes I felt as if I was invisible to her, and often I wanted to be. She'd look right at us and say, "*Some children never learn to listen. Why do I even bother?*" I had felt like shriveling into the floor. I tried to pay attention to her lessons, I really did, but my mind turned to mush around Miss Hackett. When I related this experience to Sophie, she wrinkled her brow.

"Oh, my dear," Sophie said. "I had no idea you had an experience like that. But I have to say it's an excellent illustration of how a teacher's mindset creates the weather that can either open a child's mind or shut it down. That Miss Hackett of yours is hardly a model any teacher would want to emulate."

Sophie's words struck a chord for me, though not a happy one. My worst nightmare was that I was becoming another Miss Hackett. How could this be since I wanted more than anything in the world to, well, be another Mrs. Goodwin, to have the kind of impact on my students that she had had on me. I don't remember my exact words when I shared this with Sophie. But that was the sentiment I wanted to get across.

"Thank you," Sophie said. "That means so much to me, coming from you, Emma."

"I don't mean that only as a compliment," I said. "A lot of the time I feel like I'm on a slippery slope headed toward that Judger pit. Maybe I'm more like Miss Hackett than I'd like to admit. I've got to change direction, but where do I even start with all this?"

Sophie considered this for a second, then said: "You start by cultivating the art and practice of self-observation. This practice requires your becoming more aware of certain internal signals. These signals are your own feelings, certain body sensations, your thoughts, and, of course, your moods.

"I think it would be useful for you to have an experience of the two different mindsets right now. Let's do this: I'll recite two sets of questions, each set coming from a different mindset. As I'm doing this, pay attention to how the questions impact you. Notice any little change you might feel, in your muscles, your breathing, your posture, your mood, or anything else you might become aware of."

Sophie tapped her keyboard and a list of questions popped up on her monitor. "As I recite each set of questions," Sophie said, "listen as if you were asking them of yourself. I'm going to read each question slowly. Here's the first set:

CHAPTER 3 : Mapping the Geography of Our Minds

What's wrong with me?

Why am I such a failure?

Why do awful things keep happening to me?

Whose fault is it?

Why is that person so stupid and frustrating?

Why bother?"

I listened, letting the meaning of each question sink in. I felt a slight tightening in my chest and around my shoulders, just tiny changes at first, but soon I'd begun fidgeting and twisting the rings on my fingers, a habit of mine when I'm feeling uneasy.

"Well," I said. "I'm definitely feeling tense, physically uncomfortable."

"And your mood? How would you describe what you're feeling?"

"I guess hopeless," I replied. "Definitely negative. Uptight. Pessimistic. Maybe, well, quarrelsome, defensive."

"Good," Sophie said. "Those thoughts and feelings are signals that you've stepped into Judger mindset. The more you're able to pick up on these body clues and observe your moods and thoughts, the quicker you'll be able to tell what mindset you're in. It'll get easier and easier. You might think of it as educating your observer self."

"That makes sense," I said. "But I need a way to get out of Judger."

"We're leading up to that," Sophie said. "Try this: bring to mind an incident that felt very Judger to you. But now, access your observer self and see that same situation from the perspective of sitting in this room with me, feeling safe, at ease. Imagine that Judger incident as if you are watching it like a movie. Okay?"

I nodded. The incident that came immediately to mind was the one with my student Becky, when I had tried to talk with her about her potential. At first I felt tense, with all the feelings of failure that I experienced after Becky huffed out. I was definitely in Judger mindset—about her and me. But as I shifted into observer position, watching that scene as a *movie* in my mind, those feelings began to shift, subtly at first but definitely shifting.

"Okay," I said. "I'm feeling a little more open."

"Now let's find out what happens with the Learner mindset questions."

The monitor on her desk switched to a new set of questions. Sophie reminded me to listen as if I were asking these questions of myself. Then she slowly recited the questions, pausing between each one. They sure felt different from the questions before:

What happened?

What do I want—for both myself and others?

What's useful about this event, and what can I learn?

What is the other person thinking, feeling, wanting?

What are my choices?

What's best to do now?

What's possible?

The discomfort I'd been feeling from watching that movie with Becky completely faded away. It was quickly replaced by what I can only describe as a *quiet excitement*. It was subtle at first, so I paid particular attention to my body's reactions. Gradually my breathing got easier and smoother. I felt like I was walking out into the sunlight after being in a dark room. "That's surprising," I said. "I'd never realized how much I feel words and thoughts in my body. Those Learner questions really make a difference, especially to my mood. I feel a clear distinction between being in Judger and being in Learner."

"It shows up in your physical demeanor as well as in how you think, express yourself and relate to the world," Sophie said.

Learner/Judger Questions*	
Judger	**Learner**
What's wrong with me?	What do I appreciate about me?
What's wrong with him/her?	What do I appreciate about him/her?
Whose fault is it?	Am I being responsible?
How can I prove I'm right?	What can I learn? What's useful?
Why is that person so clueless and frustrating?	What is the other person thinking, feeling, and wanting?
Haven't we been there, done that?	What are the best steps forward?
Why bother?	What's possible?

* Each of us asks ourselves and others questions from both mindsets. We also have the capacity to choose at any moment which questions will frame our thinking, listening, speaking, and relating.

"There's lots of research to back this up. For example, in his book *The Brain that Changes Itself*, Norman Doidge, a professor of neuroscience, explores how feelings, moods and beliefs impact the way the brain organizes itself.[13] Lots of people are applying this information in the classroom these days. In a very general way, Learner mindset is more positive, open, and accepting, while Judger mindset is more negative, closed, and critical. Positive moods and feelings produce a sense of wellbeing, greater attention, and more creative and holistic thinking. Contrariwise, the experience of Judger mindset is associated with more negative moods and emotions and a narrowing of attention.[14] From Judger you can't see as many options as you can from Learner, and we're mostly focused on what's wrong.

"What you just experienced, as you listened to those two sets of questions, is your capacity to recognize the two mindsets and shift from Judger to Learner. I believe this is what you gradually came to experience in the sixth grade. That shift made such a difference for you. Of course, there's a big difference between *experiencing* this kind of teaching as a young student and *applying* it in your role as a teacher years later.

"Like anything else, daily practice will make it increasingly easy to recognize the mindset you're in and choose whether or not to shift it. In time, it'll become nearly automatic, even when you're faced with difficult encounters. You're teaching your observer self to recognize and choose the mindset you bring to the classroom."

Who was I going to be when I walked into the classroom? That was the question. Did I want to be another Miss Hackett or did I want to be like Sophie?

Sophie glanced at her wristwatch. I recognized this was another kind of signal—that we were running out of time. Sophie looked a little tired, though her smile told me she had enjoyed our time together. I got up from my chair and stretched as Sophie walked over to her big mahogany table and opened one of the drawers. She pulled out a large blue folder, bulging with I knew not what, and handed it to me.

"This folder contains some handouts from my courses at the university," Sophie said. "It's all based on my doctoral research about thinking and mindsets and the questions we ask ourselves. It's work I actually started developing just a few years before you were in my class. I'm sure you'll find most of it to be self-explanatory." Next she handed me a document in a spiral binder. "These are excerpts from my personal journals," she said. "I hope to finish my writing in the next few months. It's a work in progress, and you'll find all sorts of surprises here. I'd love your feedback, Emma, and please consider today's meeting just a beginning."

Finally she handed me a beautiful, leather-bound journal.

"Here's a blank journal for your own thoughts and reflections. You may remember journaling in my class when you were a child. It's a wonderful way to reflect on what you're learning. And to transform any of your roaring tigers into kittens. Now I must rush you on your way. I've got an appointment to keep."

We said our hasty goodbyes. When we stepped out into the hall I thanked Sophie one more time, hugging her gifts to my chest.

CHAPTER 4

EXPLORING LEARNER AND
JUDGER MINDSETS

Each of us literally chooses,
by our way of attending to things,
what sort of universe we shall appear
to ourselves to inhabit.

William James

On the way home from my meeting with Sophie, I stopped to do the weekend shopping, then rushed home, put away the groceries, and got everything ready for the coming week. Jared wouldn't be back from his conference until early the next afternoon, which meant I'd have a few hours in the morning to myself. There'd be time to read over the materials Sophie had given me and make some notes in my journal. After the visit with Sophie, I had lots to write about.

Sunday morning I had a quick breakfast, made myself a mug of tea, and headed for my office. I picked up the blue folder

Sophie had given me, titled *Mindsets Make All the Difference*. There was a colorful print of Sophie's stained glass question mark on the outside of it. That image took me back to when I was twelve years old, walking into Sophie's classroom for the first time. I had stopped in my tracks, staring at that stained glass artwork with its prominent question mark. It had hung in the window by Mrs. Goodwin's big, oak teacher's desk.

Sitting in my home office and reliving that day from my childhood, I picked up the journal Sophie had given me, carefully folded back the cover and began writing. As I did, something clicked for me, creating a swirl of new connections in my brain. I wanted to capture my childhood memories on the page. I remembered how older kids from my grade school had told me that Mrs. Goodwin's class was really something special. I'd felt curious, even a bit hopeful, daring to imagine that maybe school would be different for me when she became my teacher. As my memories were reawakened, words flew from my pen, filling page after page in the journal. It was a wonderful feeling to get lost in my writing that way, starting to recall some of Sophie's early teachings. I wasn't even aware of how much time was passing.

It must have been at least an hour before I went back to explore the materials in Sophie's big blue folder. When I finally opened it up, a laminated sheet slipped from the pages and fell into my lap. I picked it up to discover it was a *Choice Map*, just like the one I'd seen on Sophie's computer screen. But it was a different experience holding it in my own hands, somehow more personal and empowering. I could settle down with the Choice Map and think about what Sophie and I had talked about at her apartment.

I propped the map up against a pile of books on my desk, then turned my attention back to the folder. In the back pocket

I found a few postcard-sized prints of the Choice Map. Great, I thought. These should come in handy. I'd put one on the refrigerator as a reminder, and maybe take some to school with me.

Next I found a two-columned sheet titled "Learner/Judger Mindset Chart." The right hand column was labeled *Learner Mindset*, the left one *Judger Mindset*. There were lists of traits for the two mindsets, such as Judger being *judgmental, reactive,* and *automatic* while Learner was *accepting, responsive,* and *thoughtful*. I remembered Sophie emphasizing that these were descriptions of people's *mindsets,* not labels for people. That made a lot of sense to me. On a good day I'm in Learner. On a bad day I'm in Judger.

The chart also showed how the two mindsets affect our *relationships,* how we're actually relating to someone at a particular moment. Judger tends to create *win/lose* relationships while Learner relationships are *win/win*. I also noticed that Judger was associated with feeling separate from others, while Learner was associated with feeling connected with other people. I also saw that our mindsets affect the way we *listen*.

I remember how I had felt in Sophie's class. Those words *accepting, responsive,* and *thoughtful* described how I'd felt having Sophie as my teacher. She created a sense of *connectedness* that had put me at ease—just the opposite of how I'd felt in school before that (more like the proverbial deer in the headlights). As Sophie had pointed out, when we're feeling threatened, we tend to react in one of three ways: we want to run, fight, or freeze. I mostly froze.

In Sophie's class I didn't freeze. Well, maybe I did at first, but after a while, I had begun feeling safe, and even looked forward to school. My mind had begun working in ways it had rarely done with other teachers.

As I studied Sophie's Learner/Judger Mindset Chart I

Learner/Judger Mindsets*

Judger Mindset	Learner Mindset
Judgmental (of people and facts)	Accepting (of people and facts)
Reactive and automatic	Responsive and thoughtful
Critical	Appreciative
More close-minded	More open-minded
Know-it-all, self-righteous	Comfortable with not-knowing
Blame oriented	Responsibility oriented
Own point of view only	Takes multiple perspectives
Inflexible and rigid	Flexible and adaptive
Either/or thinking	Both/and thinking
Defends assumptions	Questions assumptions
Mistakes are bad	Mistakes are to learn from
Presumes scarcity	Presumes sufficiency
Possibilities seen as limited	Possibilities seen as unlimited
Primary mood: protective	Primary mood: curious

Learner/Judger Relationships*

Judger Relationships	Learner Relationships
Win-lose relating	Win-win relating
Dismissive, maybe demeaning	Discerning, accepting
Positional conversation	Collaborative conversation
Separate from self/others	Connected with self/others
Fears difference	Values difference
Feedback considered rejection	Feedback considered worthwhile
Destructive conflict	Constructive conflict
Judger ears listen for:	Learner ears listen for:
What's wrong about person and their opinion	What's valuable about person and their opinion
Agree or disagree	Understanding
Danger	Possibility
Seeks to attack or is defensive	Seeks to appreciate, resolve and create

**Each of us has both mindsets and always will. We each have the capacity to choose where we relate from in any moment.

began applying it to the problems I'd been having at school. What would it tell me about my relationship with Becky? I'd already seen that I was mostly in Judger with her. But what were the specifics? How could I better understand the mindset I brought to that relationship? My eyes shot to the part about *listening* toward the bottom of the chart. What was the quality of my listening? Was I listening to Becky the way Sophie had listened to me? Well, I couldn't deny that I usually focused on what was *wrong* with Becky. Sure, she had written four excellent sentences in that essay, but mostly what she wrote *was* a real mess. She wasn't taking the time to be a good student. I remembered something Sophie had said about *generous listening* and began to feel uncomfortable. Was I listening to Becky seeking to *understand* her better? She sure wasn't behaving as if I were. To the contrary, she acted defensively, as though I was attacking her. In our relationship, Becky wasn't winning, nor was I.

What was going on here? This was just the opposite of the experience I had always imagined having with my students. Then it hit me. Becky was almost a mirror image of *me* at that age! How many times as I was growing up did I ask myself: *What's wrong with me?* And then I recalled Miss Hackett's words: "Why can't you see how much potential you have, Emma? There are children who would give anything to have your intelligence. Why are you wasting it?" Her words had made me feel terrible. What was wrong with me that I not only wasted this *potential* thing she talked about, I couldn't even figure out what it was!

I looked at that chart again and reflected on the relationship Sophie established with me and her other students in our class. I always felt that she listened with deep understanding: responsive, and interested in our questions, perspectives, and differences. The primary mood, what she'd called the *weather*, in the class, was one of respect, openness, and curiosity. She was just so inviting. What a contrast to Miss Hackett's rigid and judgmental ways! Hackett patrolled the classroom, waiting to pounce on anyone who said or did anything wrong. Sophie wasn't like that at all. You could always tell that she expected us to have something worthwhile to say.

I had just picked up Sophie's Choice Map again when I heard Jared's car pulling into the driveway. I glanced at my watch. He was almost two hours late! His key rattled in the lock, the front door burst open, and he dashed down the hall like a storm-trooper, right past my office door. Seconds later he was on the kitchen phone, sounding very professional, though I knew darn well he was upset about something.

I stepped into the kitchen as he was hanging up the phone.

"Are you okay?" I asked.

"Oh, Emma," he said. "It's been a hellish day. It seems like nothing went right. You know that guy at work who . . . oh, let's not talk about it now." He took my two hands in his, pulled me to him, and gave me a quick hug and kiss. His shoulders were knotted with tension. This was not the time to talk with him about my problems.

He opened the refrigerator, grabbed the bottle of orange juice, and filled a glass for each of us. We went to the living room, plopped down on our faded old sofa, and he kicked off his shoes.

"On top of everything else, my plane was late," he said, "my cell phone died at the airport, I missed an important call, and then spent an hour looking for the ticket to get my car out of the parking lot." He turned to me with a self-deprecating grin. "I hope your day went better than mine."

We sat in silence for a minute or two, lost in our own thoughts. He relaxed a bit and put his arm around my shoulder. That's when he noticed the Choice Map I was still holding in my hand.

"What's that?"

"I got it from Sophie yesterday," I said, adding that our meeting had been wonderful.

He took the Choice Map from my hand and perused it with considerable interest, reading aloud as he did: "*Learner Mindset. Judger Mindset. Switching Lane. What assumptions am I making? Whose fault is it? Am I being responsible? What's wrong with them? What are my choices?* Hunh. You know, this makes a lot of sense to me. It really does."

He began asking questions about the map and I explained as best I could, trying to remember Sophie's explanations.

"I get it," Jared said, following what I said with his finger on the map. "I only wish I'd had this with me this weekend. It lays things out so clearly and simply. How many times a day do I ask questions that take me down that dead-end street . . ."

"To the Judger pit," I said, finishing his sentence for him.

"If I understand what this map is illustrating," he said, "it's a way of tracing out where our thoughts are taking us throughout the day."

"Yes, that's exactly it." I paused, then asked, "Do you think you ever get stuck in Judger mindset, I mean really stuck?"

He twisted toward me on the sofa. "You're joking, aren't you—after the way I stormed in here this afternoon? Of course I get stuck in Judger."

"Okay. You're forgiven," I said brightly. "I'm glad I'm not the only one."

His face suddenly got very serious. "Sweetheart," he said, "we need to talk about something. Maybe this map will help." He paused and took my hand. "It has to do with your being unhappy with your job. After that talk we had in the car, I started asking myself, what would happen if you gave up being a teacher? Your passion for teaching was one of the first things that attracted me to you. When you talked about teaching, your voice changed, and your face lit up in a special way. Your excitement really fascinated me. I knew you were sharing an important part of yourself, something quite precious and rare.

"I loved hearing you tell about the kids in your practice teaching, when they suddenly had breakthroughs and solved problems that had been giving them trouble, or when you helped a kid discover some ability he didn't even know he had. I loved hearing about things you were learning to help those kids. It was like you possessed this special magic to turn on their brains. I felt really privileged. Nobody had ever shared things like that with me before. So you see, your dream of being a teacher is pretty important to me, too. I realize it's a lot different now. You're not practice teaching anymore. You've got your own classroom, with different responsibilities and pressures. And I realize that it's not exactly like back in college. But the idea that you'd give all that up is . . . well, it worries me. Don't you see? If you gave all that up, I'd be losing something really important to me, too. Is that selfish of me? Your passion about being a teacher is so much about who you are, about the woman I fell in love with. What would it mean to *us,* if you quit?" He paused, looking down at the floor dejectedly.

I felt tears welling up in my eyes. It had never occurred to me that giving up my personal dream would have such an impact on my husband. I had to admit it was kind of startling how he described me, and how deeply he'd been affected by what I'd shared with him. Another thought immediately intruded, and my body tensed up: deciding to quit or stay in teaching was my own private choice, wasn't it? What Jared told me piled more pressure on me. Still, if I couldn't be a teacher who could make a real difference in my students' lives, a teacher like Sophie, then I'd better get out of the way and make room for teachers who *could.*

"And then there are the practical issues involved," I heard Jared say.

"Practical issues?" Those words jolted me. I wanted to stop this conversation before it escalated into something messy.

"We rented this house and bought a new car last year," he said. "To say nothing of the fact that we're both still paying off student loans! We've made certain decisions, thinking we would have two decent salaries we could depend on," he said. "What's going to happen if you quit and can't find another job?"

I immediately felt myself getting defensive and sliding into Judger. Why did Jared have to come down on me so hard? Didn't he realize what I was going through? Was he going to see me as a big nothing if I washed out as a teacher? I didn't know what to do or say, so I did what I'd always done before Sophie came into my life: I froze up and kept my mouth shut.

"I don't know how to help," Jared was saying. "But I do know that the look in your eyes when you talked about being a teacher came from a special place within you. You don't just walk away from something that important. It would break both our hearts. Teaching has got to be one of the toughest professions in the world. Considering this Choice Map and what you've told me about Sophie, I'm sure she could help you through this. Meanwhile, I don't want to hide things from you, like how your self-doubts impacted me the other day."

Jared's eyes told me how true this was. My self-doubts really did have an impact on him. "Don't worry," I told him, touching his chin with my fingertip. "I've done a lot of thinking since my visit with Sophie. I do still want to be a teacher. The trouble is, I just don't know how to make it work for me yet."

Jared set the Choice Map on the end table and we slid into each other's arms. His smile told me that he'd really meant everything he said about my dream—and about what it meant to both of us.

CHAPTER 5

THINKING WITH NEW QUESTIONS

Everything we know has its origins in questions.
Questions, we might say, are the principal
intellectual instruments available to human beings.

Neil Postman

When I arrived at my classroom on Monday morning, I went immediately to the teachers' bulletin board just to the right of the door. That was where we posted everything from emergency phone numbers to a calendar of school holidays and the weekly schedules of staff meetings. Right in the middle, dominating the board, was Dr. Malstrom's Behavior Chart. I cringed. Every child in the class knew what it meant when I walked over to that chart holding—or, in Mrs. Santiago's case, *brandishing*—a big black marking pen. It meant that somebody was going to get a big X next to their name, and this would tell the world they were in trouble for misbehaving in class. When they got three Xs in a week, they would be sent to the principal's office. Though Dr. Malstrom had retired, I'm afraid some of her antiquated ways lived on. Every time I made a mark on that chart, I was reminded of Miss Hackett. Maybe she didn't use a chart exactly like this one, but she had her own way of punishing and humiliating us. Every time I used that odious chart of Dr. Malstrom's, I could feel my stomach knot up.

I reached into my purse and pulled out one of the postcard-sized Choice Maps I'd brought from home. I made a place for it right next to the Behavior Chart where it would remind me of Sophie's teachings. If one of these days I got rid of that Behavior Chart, would Mrs. Santiago make a big fuss about it? I bristled when I thought of how Mrs. Santiago's ways of doing things impacted how I felt just walking into the classroom each morning. I was hoping Sophie's teachings would help, but in the meantime I was still feeling pretty stuck.

I walked over to my desk, sat down, and began correcting some tests from the previous week, trying not to let my feelings about Mrs. Santiago distract me. Sure, I recognized those feelings were mainly Judger, but that's just the way it was for the time being.

A few minutes later, when Mrs. Santiago arrived, I greeted her with admittedly a forced smile. Even a forced smile was better than a scowl, I figured.

It was Mrs. Santiago's habit to walk around the room looking for anything that was out of order, inspecting the desktops to see if they had been properly cleaned by the janitors the night before. If she saw spots or smears, she got out a bottle of spray cleaner, a handful of paper towels, and redid the job herself. She said it was an important message to the kids. I sometimes worried that she wanted to point that spray cleaner at me. She completed her inspections, apparently pleased with what she found.

She walked over to the teachers' bulletin board to check for any notices. I sometimes left memos for her there, such as notices if a child would be absent or late that day, or if there was a special staff meeting scheduled. She stopped and put on her reading glasses, kept handy on a silver chain around her neck. She leaned closer to inspect the Choice Map. After a while she turned around, caught my eye, and started to say something. Just then a group of five children burst into the room and she focused her attention on greeting them, reminding them about using their classroom voices.

Amid the sounds of children's voices, chairs scraping over the floor as everyone took their seats, and books being plopped onto the tables, the room slowly began to settle down. Mrs. Santiago took her place at the front of the room. It was her day to get things started. She greeted everyone, made a couple of announcements, and asked if anyone had something to share with the class.

For some reason, the kids were unusually reticent that morning. When that happens, I always try to have a story of my own ready, so I briefly told them about my meeting with Mrs. Goodwin, who had been my teacher in the sixth grade. I told them that she had become *Doctor* Goodwin since then, but that she would always be Mrs. Goodwin to me. Hands flew up as soon as I was finished.

"I bet she's a really old lady by now, isn't she," one boy remarked.

"Oh, she's not that old," I said, smiling as I recalled how, when I was in the sixth grade, anyone over thirty had seemed ancient. "But she's probably as old as your grandma."

"My grandma is really sick," the boy said sadly.

"I'll bet you were an all-A student," another child piped up.

"To tell the truth," I said, "I had a difficult time with school for quite a while. Until Mrs. Goodwin's class I never got an A on my report card, but more importantly, for the first time in my life I started to love being a student. With her as my teacher, I truly started *learning how to learn*. She taught us how to ask questions that got our minds working in ways they never had before. After that I did very well in school."

"And that's why you're a teacher now, isn't it?" a girl named Deborah asked.

Her question gave me pause. Yes, I had done very well in school but like Jared had said, there were other things that had drawn me into teaching. Maybe I could change lives as Sophie Goodwin had changed mine. I glanced over at Mrs. Santiago a little nervously. She smiled back and shrugged stiffly.

"That's an interesting question," I told Deborah. "I'll have to think about it."

"Teacher?" I almost missed the soft voice that came from the table near the middle of the room. It took me a second to locate Becky's half-raised hand.

"Yes, Becky," I said, delighted to see that she was participating. I couldn't remember the last time she'd spoken up in class without my or Mrs. Santiago's prompting.

"What's that little thing up there?" Becky pointed at the teachers' bulletin board.

I walked over and placed my finger on the border of the Choice Map. "Do you mean this? It's called a Choice Map. Mrs. Goodwin gave it to me. It's about...well...it helps us make choices about the kinds of questions we ask ourselves and how we think." I stopped, realizing I was feeling insecure about explaining mindsets to the class. Besides, would Mrs. Santiago think I was wasting study time?

"Can I ask another question?" Becky asked.

"Of course," I said.

"Is it like the Behavior Chart?" Becky got an expression on her face that I'd seen many times before with other kids, halfway between anger and tears. She squinched up her eyes and wrinkled her nose.

I was taken aback. "No, not at all. It's a reminder to me of some of the wonderful things I learned in the sixth grade," I answered quickly.

Becky suddenly relaxed. "You mean when you learned to learn?" she asked. She now had that open-faced look children get when they've discovered something surprising and intriguing.

"Yes," I said. "And it made all the difference in the world."

I wanted to say more, but I was momentarily speechless. One of the things that had drawn me to teaching was the way kids come up with such delightfully surprising questions. Sometimes those questions inspired a very different way of thinking about a problem or, as Sophie might have said, those questions came from curiosity and Learner mindset.

Mrs. Santiago, always aware of the ticking clock and our lesson plans, stepped in. She didn't exactly interrupt, but I gave her the floor, knowing we needed to keep things moving. Still, as I sat down, I caught myself feeling resentful. I would have loved to keep talking about the Choice Map, exploring questions the kids raised. Instead, I took out my attendance roster and checked over each name, making sure I had noted the three absences. As I did I vaguely followed Mrs. Santiago's exchanges with the children. Together they reviewed what they'd been working on last Friday and she gave them prompts that brought them up to speed with what we had planned for today.

By eleven-thirty, when we broke for lunch and the kids scurried off to the cafeteria, we'd completed everything in the morning's lesson plans. As I was putting away some materials we'd been using, I noticed Mrs. Santiago standing by the bulletin board again.

"I'm sorry," I said, looking up. "Were you waiting for me?"

I realized I was already in Judger mindset and preparing to defend myself for posting the Choice Map.

"I have some questions about this map of yours," she said.

Oh, boy, I thought. Here it comes. I didn't feel like hearing her complaints. Why, I wondered, did she resist anything new? And why did she think she had to stick with the old ways she'd learned from her mentor, Mrs. Peterson? She needed to accept the fact that I was, after all, the senior teacher here, even though I was younger. My shoulders stiffened and my jaw tightened.

"I'd be glad to discuss the Choice Map with you," I said. "Maybe we could take some time this afternoon, after class." I knew this would have to be a short meeting because every Monday she had to pick up her niece at the high school and take her to drama class at the community center.

"I was hoping we could discuss it during lunch," Mrs. Santiago said. "I'm quite intrigued by this map. Something tells me it's very important."

"You're really interested?" I asked, flabbergasted.

"Of course I am," she said. "We're way overdue on changing that dreadful Behavior Chart, if that's what you're planning."

"Well, sure," I stammered, realizing how I'd miscalculated her response. "Do you really think it can replace the Behavior Chart?"

"Isn't that what you're planning? Every time we put an X on that Behavior Chart, I swear half the class heads toward this Judger pit that's drawn on your map here." She pointed at the drawing of the Judger pit. "I don't think we learn much that way, not really. Do you? It just makes the kids feel bad about themselves. And it makes me feel bad, too."

I was nearly speechless. "How did you figure that out so quickly?"

Mrs. Santiago pointed at the Choice Map. "I read the questions over the heads of those figures on the Judger path," she answered. "That's how our kids look whenever we put Xs by their names. And I'll bet the questions they ask themselves are like the ones in the bubbles." She paused. "Mrs. Peterson was a wonderful teacher. I owe her a lot. But I'm not her, and I can't keep trying to teach like her. Some of her teaching methods don't fit me very well anymore." She shrugged. "Maybe they never did. As for Dr. Malstrom, she was a strict disciplinarian of the old school. Maybe her Behavior Chart served its purpose in her time."

I couldn't have been more surprised. All the time we'd taught together, she'd never mentioned these things. I felt like hugging her.

"It's a beautiful day outside," I said. "Let's get our lunches and go out to the picnic tables at the back of the playground. I'd love to tell you about Sophie Goodwin."

We had both brought sandwiches from home. We grabbed what we needed and hurried across the playground to the lunch area, under a covering of trees. Most of the kids had run off to play, leaving the area to the two of us.

I got out my thermos of coffee and two small Choice Maps from my purse, handing one of them to Mrs. Santiago. A few moments later, we were discussing Learner and Judger mindsets. I couldn't explain the ideas as well as Sophie did but I could feel that something important was happening between Mrs. Santiago and me. I was able to see how open and curious she was. If Sophie had been there, I'm sure she would've said I was seeing Mrs. Santiago through Learner eyes rather than Judger ones, maybe for the first time.

Over lunch, we started coming up with ways we might use the Choice Map to replace the Behavior Chart, or at least start in that direction. We both wondered how the kids would react to that change. Did some kids really need Dr. Malstrom's system to teach them there were consequences to their actions? And were some kids motivated by getting stars after their names? Didn't we need a way to track children who acted out?

We even started speculating about how the old Behavior Chart affected the *weather* in our classroom. Mrs. Santiago loved that concept. "I know that Behavior Chart stirs up little storms rather than creating a climate for learning," she said. "Do you think Dr. Marshall will be okay with our throwing out the Behavior Chart?"

"Somehow, I think he will," I said. Then I told her how he'd known Sophie, too, and about how Sophie's mentoring and research about mindsets and questioning had helped him change the direction his life had been going.

As we walked back toward our classroom, Mrs. Santiago said, "This is all very exciting. Maybe he could ask Dr. Goodwin to give a presentation to all the teachers."

"Great idea," I said. "I'll ask him, for sure."

Our conversation that day made me realize I'd been totally misjudging Mrs. Santiago, and this worried me. If my perceptions of her had been off by that much, what else had I been distorting with my Judger mindset? As I was opening the classroom door, she said something that stopped me in my tracks.

"When I first met you," she said, "I was really intimidated. You're so young, with so many fresh new ideas, and you graduated from one of the best education departments in the state. I didn't think I'd ever be able to keep up with you. Most of my training was under Mrs. Peterson, as you know. She was very different from you or me. I have so much to learn from you."

Then I *did* hug her. "I guess we've misread each other. I was intimidated by *you* because I thought you'd see me as just another one of those smart-aleck college kids with a big chip on my shoulder. I was sure you were stuck in the ways you learned from Mrs. Peterson. This Choice Map has given us both new perspectives. I'm really grateful for it."

For the rest of the day I felt like I was living in a different world. The *weather* was *definitely* changing for me. How could I have missed what I'd discovered about Mrs. Santiago today? Without realizing it, I'd been spending way too much time in Judger territory. Had I actually been coming across like another Miss Hackett? Was that really possible? No wonder Mrs. Santiago had been intimidated by me. With questions like these, Sophie's Choice Map had started working miracles that day.

At the end of that day, while Mrs. Santiago and I were straightening up the classroom and getting it ready for the next day, we talked again. She told me that she had dreamed of being a teacher since she was a small child. She'd had wonderful teachers, she said. She always looked up to them as leaders and sources of hope. Her family hadn't been able to afford to send her to college so she'd taken night and summer courses for years. "I was lucky enough to get a job as a teaching assistant," she said, "so that I could be in the classroom and help children learn."

That day was a huge breakthrough for both of us. We decided to start writing down new questions about more constructive ways to address students' behavior problems. What did those kids who were always acting out need from us? What were they thinking, feeling, and wanting? What was the big picture that we were perhaps missing? What was possible? What would work? Mrs. Santiago nodded enthusiastically, then rushed off to take her niece to her drama class.

As I was leaving school a few minutes later, I passed Dr. Marshall's open door and he called out to me.

"Oh, Emma, I'm so glad I caught you," he said. "How did the meeting with Dr. Goodwin go? She sent me an e-mail thanking me for the reconnection with you. What did she mean by that? She said you'd tell me all about it."

"You really didn't know?" I exclaimed. "Mrs. Goodwin was my teacher in the sixth grade."

Dr. Marshall's jaw dropped. "I had no idea," he said.

"She's a miracle worker," I said. "But of course, you already know that."

He laughed. "Yes, she is a bit of a miracle worker, isn't she? Except for one thing. She's proven that what looks like a miracle is actually quite teachable; it's not some unique power of hers. I'm living proof of her work being teachable. Her work on mindsets and questions has made a huge difference in my life. If I hadn't taken her course at the university, I doubt I would have stayed in education. I owe a lot to her."

After telling Dr. Marshall about my meeting with Sophie, I told him about the breakthrough Mrs. Santiago and I had that day. He listened intently, nodding and smiling as I shared the news with him. At the end of our conversation he congratulated me on my progress, and I went on to the parking lot with a new glow. What an amazing day it had been.

When I got home, I couldn't wait to call Sophie. I told her about the meeting with Mrs. Santiago, and how we had been talking about using the Choice Map to replace that Behavior Chart, or somehow make it less odious. I asked if she had suggestions for us.

"Well," she said, "dealing with behavior problems is a dilemma that all teachers have to wrestle with. We want kids to be accountable for their actions and we certainly can't permit behavior that makes it difficult for other children to learn. In the best of all worlds, each child would develop *internal controls* rather than having control imposed from the outside. That's a big part of what the Choice Map is about—teaching those internal controls."

"For some of today's classroom problems that can be a huge order," I said.

"Oh, there's no doubt about it," Sophie said. "But when our efforts are backed up with tools that work, I don't think we're being unrealistic. Learning to be accountable for our own actions is fundamental, whether it's in our interactions with others or with our intellectual pursuits. One doesn't develop excellence, or maybe even competence, without it."

"I agree," I said. "That Behavior Chart doesn't achieve anything but temporary and resentful compliance at best."

"As you develop your skills with the Learner mindset tools," Sophie said, "you'll feel less drained by having to police your students' behavior, and you'll begin noticing the weather changing in the classroom. You'll be able to put more of your energy into teaching, into helping your students experience their own innate capacities, develop their intellectual abilities and express themselves creatively and collaboratively. This is where you find the deepest rewards of being a teacher. It won't happen right away. This approach isn't a magic pill but there is a certain magic in it.

"Carefully observe your students and the results you're getting by using the Behavior Chart. What would you think, feel, or do differently if you were referencing the Choice Map instead? To what extent is it necessary to control behavior for the sake of maintaining order and a sense of safety in the classroom? How do we do this, and still help children become self-actualized and skillful? Just keep asking the kinds of questions you and Mrs. Santiago are asking. Write about what you observe, using your journal. Stay forever curious. And schedule regular times when you and Mrs. Santiago can discuss what you're observing and what you're learning."

"That breakthrough with Mrs. Santiago today never would

have been possible without your help," I told Sophie. "It all started with putting that little copy of the Choice Map on the bulletin board."

Sophie said, "You know, I'd love to visit your classroom and meet Mrs. Santiago, if it wouldn't be an imposition. I have to be down your way in about two weeks for some tests. I could slip into your class to visit in the afternoon. Would that be okay with you?"

I could hardly believe my ears. "I'll check it with Mrs. Santiago, but I'm sure she'll be delighted."

As exciting as it was to contemplate Sophie's visit, I have to confess I was nervous about it, too, afraid she'd see what an amateur I was compared to her.

That evening when Jared got home, I could hardly wait to share my news with him. He would be relieved to hear I was actually getting enthusiastic about school. But before I was able to tell him, he said he had news of his own.

"A strange thing happened today," Jared said. "I pinned that little map you gave me on my cubicle wall. Then Mickey Stonewell—that's the guy from marketing I've complained about—stopped by to give me some reports. As he was leaving he noticed the Choice Map, and jabbed his finger at it. Then he leaned over and in a loud, sarcastic voice, started reeling off those questions in the little bubbles over those figures on the Judger path. I don't think he even noticed the Learner path.

"I was bracing myself, as I usually do, because he bugs me so much. I wanted to tell him to shove off. Talk about being in Judger! But then I thought about the Learner path and asked myself what's happening here? What do I want? What assumptions am I making about Mickey? What can I learn about him? What's going on with him? And what are my choices?

"I realized that something had to change between us or we

were headed for a big blowup. We have to get along or neither of us can do our jobs. If I ever hoped to develop a decent working relationship with this guy I'd have to take off my Judger ears and start listening with Learner ears. We'll have to wait and see how it plays out but I'm already feeling more open about my next meeting with him. That's what matters for now."

"*Listening with Learner ears*," I echoed. "I love that!"

Jared looked a little puzzled.

"That's brilliant," I said. "That's what I've started doing with Mrs. Santiago, listening with Learner ears, and it's begun to change everything."

I'd never thought about actually *choosing how I listened.* That notion made me wonder how I'd been listening to Becky, Brandon, and all my other students for that matter. Jared's story raised a whole new set of questions for me to think about.

CHAPTER 6

LISTENING WITH LEARNER EARS

My words itch at your ears till you understand them . . .
Walt Whitman

Mrs. Santiago and I started having regular meetings, sometimes for a few minutes at the end of the day, sometimes over lunch. As I shared more of Sophie's materials with her, our exchanges became increasingly collaborative and creative. There were other changes, too. Good ones. We were now on a first name basis: Carmen and Emma. I'd never called her anything but Mrs. Santiago before.

One afternoon, after the children had left, Carmen showed me a sheet of paper she'd found crumpled up on the floor near Brandon's desk. She smiled uneasily as she smoothed it out on the desk for me to see.

Scrawled at the top in blocky letters were the words *Behavior Chart,* except that Behavior was misspelled: *Behaver.* Under that were two names: my own and Carmen's. Following each of our names were long rows of Xs. Carmen watched as I examined the paper. Earlier in the day we'd both put Xs after Brandon's name on the Behavior Chart, mostly for his obnoxious remarks about other kids. He talked more than any other child in the class, but most of it had little to do with any lessons. Much of the time he was interrupting other people, including Carmen and me. There were times when he didn't seem able to contain himself.

While I had never seen Brandon get physically abusive or bully other children, he was verbally aggressive and could certainly be intimidating. Other kids gave him a wide berth, making me wonder if they were afraid of him. When he tried to join in their conversations they often snubbed him. Then he got an angry look on his face that I was pretty sure covered up hurt feelings. In class, when other children were speaking, he sometimes made derisive remarks slightly above a whisper: "That's stupid!" Or, "Duh!" Or something worse. Every time this happened I pictured that famous Norman Rockwell painting of a teacher marching a misbehaving student out of the classroom by his ear. I never would have done that, of course, though I was certainly tempted. Thankfully, the threat of getting another X on the Behavior Chart was usually enough to keep him in line.

"I guess he was giving us a taste of our own medicine," I told Carmen, pointing to the Behavior Chart Brandon had drawn. I thought about this for a moment, then added, "At the end of the day, I sometimes feel just like this, that I'm on everybody's Behavior Chart with a bunch of Xs after my name. What if I'm becoming another Miss Hackett?"

Carmen looked puzzled. "Miss Hackett?"

"She's the teacher who made my life so miserable in the fifth grade. If all my teachers had been like her I would have flunked out of school and grown up believing I was nothing but a lump, with no brain at all. My worst fear is that I might come across like Miss Hackett, and hurt my students the way she did me."

"I know what you mean," Carmen said. "It's what I call my 'Wicked Witch of the West' days. When I look at this Behavior Chart of Brandon's I start going Judger on myself, too. I remember what I was like at his age. See, I got teased mercilessly because of my accent. And I got so embarrassed when I couldn't remember the right word for something in English! It was humiliating. When I felt really bad, I took it out on Armando, my little brother. I was pretty mean to him sometimes. Somebody should have put a whole lot of Xs by my name for the way I acted toward him."

"When we go Judger on Brandon," I reflected, "we aren't creating the kind of classroom we want, for him or the other kids, either. I just don't know what else to do. Sophie says it's our response to our students that determines whether a crisis is escalated or de-escalated. I'm afraid Brandon's drawing of the Behavior Chart tells us that we need to learn some *de-escalating* tactics. I'm pretty sure you can only de-escalate things from Learner mindset. But how do we do that and still maintain control of the classroom?"

"I don't know," Carmen said. "But lately, whenever I apply things I'm learning from that Learner/Judger Chart of Sophie's, I've noticed certain small changes with Brandon and with a couple of the other kids. I try to listen from Learner and not just automatically go Judger when somebody misbehaves. It had never occurred to me that the mindset with which I'm listening could affect so much of what I take in or understand. I don't think I'm imagining things when I say that I'm having better luck with Brandon, not all the time, but at least now and then. He's being much more responsive with me."

"Maybe it's like Sophie says," I contemplated. "It really does make all the difference when we feel *received* and *respected*, *heard* and *valued*, and that our thoughts and feelings matter to other people."

Carmen raised an eyebrow. *"Saber de escuchar,"* Carmen said. "Become a good listener."

"My husband Jared calls it 'Learner ears.' He says that by listening with Learner ears he's developing a better relationship with this guy at work who really annoys him. Good question to ask, don't you think? Am I listening with Learner ears or Judger ears?"

Am I listening with Learner ears or Judger ears?

"It's true," Carmen said. "The teachers who made the biggest difference in my life were all wonderful listeners. They never made us feel wrong, even when they were correcting us or teaching us a better way to act in class. They always made me feel valued and heard. But they didn't put up with any nonsense. Maybe they didn't use the same words as your friend Dr. Goodwin uses but I think they were doing something similar, in their own ways."

"But you can't be nice all the time," I said, thinking about Brandon. "You've got to stop disruptive behavior. The trick is how to do that without *escalating* the problem, and in a way that prevents future acting out. One thing I know for sure, that Behavior Chart and everything it symbolizes is all about Judger, and nothing about Learner. It focuses only on what kids do wrong and shows nothing about what they do right. It doesn't help them *learn* how to change their behavior. How do we create a Learner climate in our classroom?"

"Yes," Carmen said. "The question is, how do we create a classroom climate that fosters our kids' Learner mindsets, so they can develop more personal responsibility, self-control and self-discipline?"

We talked for another twenty minutes or so after that, but I can't remember everything we covered. That little Behavior Chart that Brandon had drawn opened up a new dialogue, a whole new set of questions for Carmen and me. Maybe we hadn't come up with any solutions yet but I was sure we were on the right track. After she left I took some time to write in my journal:

> Maybe listening with Learner ears can promote feelings of connectedness with our students, just as Jared described with that guy he works with and as Carmen and I discussed today. And look at how different my relationship is with Carmen since we started listening to each other with our Learner mindsets.
>
> What are some questions that Learner ears might listen with? Maybe, "What's interesting or valuable about what this student is saying?" Judger ears might wonder, "What's stupid or irrelevant about what this student is saying?" Here's a really scary thought. If I'm listening with Judger ears with my students, how might that affect their ability to learn and even what grades they get . . .

That night I called Sophie and told her about Brandon's Behavior Chart and the conversation Carmen and I had had about it.

"That chart of his is a perfect symbol, isn't it?" Sophie said.

"What do you mean?" I was puzzled.

"It's a symbol of the challenges of trying to change others when we're in Judger ourselves," she replied. "Remember that Judger begets Judger and Learner begets Learner. Of course, it can be necessary to contain unacceptable or destructive behavior with the threat of harsh consequences. It's just a fact of life in schools these days, even in the lower grades. There aren't any easy answers for managing the classroom. But it always comes down to our own responsibility for creating the weather anyway, doesn't it? One thing we do know, you don't create a climate for learning with Judger attitudes and behavior. It just can't work that way."

Judger begets Judger and Learner begets Learner.

I told her Jared's story about his co-worker Mickey and that phrase he had used, "listening with Learner ears," and she loved it as much as Carmen and I did. She said she couldn't wait to tell her graduate students about it.

"If you keep this up," Sophie said, "I might end up asking you to help me finish writing my workbook."

On that note, we reconfirmed her visit to my classroom the next day and I said how much I was looking forward to introducing her to our students. After we hung up I started wondering, had Sophie been serious about helping with her workbook? Probably I was reading too much into what she said. Did I dare let myself even imagine that she really meant it?

The afternoon of Sophie's visit she tiptoed in quietly and took a chair in the back. Not too surprisingly, the children seemed to barely notice her; entering a room like that seems to be a trick teachers develop from years of classroom experience.

After we'd finished our lessons, Sophie gave a little nod in my direction and I knew she was ready for me to introduce her to the class. She walked to the front of the room, thanked me for inviting her, smiled at the children and said hello to them. As she stood there, her very presence was welcoming, and I could see that the children were captivated by her. Her very presence took command of the classroom. I was totally in awe. It was as if she had known these kids for a lifetime.

"Dr. Goodwin," I told the class, "was my own sixth grade teacher. Some of you will remember that I told you about her."

"I've got a question," Brandon said, waving his arm wildly, and sitting on the edge of his seat to make certain he'd be noticed.

"Yes, sir," Sophie said, focusing her attention on him.

"Did Mrs. Shepherd ever get bad marks on your Behavior Chart?"

Carmen and I exchanged glances. I wasn't at all sure what Brandon was up to. How was Sophie going to handle this? But she didn't miss a beat.

"You know what," Sophie told Brandon. "I don't know your name." She walked up to him and extended her hand. He puffed up his chest and answered politely: "It's Brandon. I'm named after my uncle Brandon."

The two of them shook hands.

"But what about Mrs. Shepherd?" Brandon asked. "Is it true that she wasn't always a good student? Did she get in trouble?"

"Let's ask her," Sophie said. "I'm sure she'll be able to answer you better than I could."

Brandon glanced nervously from Sophie to me, then back to Sophie.

"I wasn't a great student until Dr. Goodwin's class," I said. "I never knew how to actually *be* a good student before that. But I don't think I gave anybody much trouble. And besides, we didn't have a Behavior Chart. I guess the most trouble I gave her was that I didn't talk a lot. I always thought I was pretty dumb." I paused for a moment to think, then added, "She taught me it wasn't dumb to ask questions."

CHAPTER 6 : Listening with Learner Ears

I wondered if I should be sharing such personal information with him. What would he do with it?

"You're not dumb," Brandon exclaimed. "That's really stupid. Anybody who thinks you're dumb is really stupid."

Laughter rippled through the class.

"Shut up," Brandon said. He looked around the room daring anyone to challenge him. "That's not funny."

"I agree," Sophie said, taking a few steps closer to Brandon. "It's not funny. But I'm curious. What questions would you have asked Mrs. Shepherd when she was a girl in my sixth grade? You know, if you knew she was smart and she thought she was dumb—what would you have asked her?"

Brandon wrinkled his brow. The whole class fell silent, waiting for his response. "I don't know," he said finally, looking quite dejected. Suddenly he turned around and snapped at a boy sitting directly behind him. "Who are you looking at? You don't know any questions either."

"Okay, guys," Sophie said. "Settle down. Remember, Mrs. Shepherd really was a girl your age back then, and if she says she thought she was dumb, she must have believed it."

"But she wasn't dumb," Brandon said. "I just can't think of any questions for her."

I halfway expected Carmen to walk over to the Behavior Chart but she just kept watching Brandon intently.

Finally he said: "Do you mean questions like, what makes you so scared? Or maybe it's like, why are you so scared of letting anybody know how smart you are?"

"That's great," Sophie said. "Those are very deep questions. I like that. I wonder how many people ask *themselves* questions like that."

Brandon glanced over his shoulder and made eye contact with Becky. Then Becky looked down. I'd never realized the two of them were friends but that exchange between them was unmistakable.

"Sometimes I do," Brandon said. "Yeah. But you don't say it out loud because they'll get mad."

"I agree," Sophie said. "Sometimes you have to ask yourself questions in your own mind, as if they were secrets you weren't quite ready to tell. When Mrs. Sheppard was my student, I might have asked myself, 'What does she want? What does she need? How can I be most helpful to her?' Or maybe I asked myself, 'What's wonderful about her that she doesn't realize yet?'" Sophie maintained eye contact with Brandon as she explained this.

"Just because you don't talk, doesn't mean you're dumb," Brandon said.

"What did she answer when you asked those questions?" one of the girls asked Sophie.

"Oh, I was asking *myself* those questions, not out loud," Sophie said. "You know, I was just thinking them in my own mind."

"What good is that?" Brandon asked. "If you don't have any answers, you shouldn't be asking so many questions all the time."

Sophie smiled at him and said, "Oh, I'd say something a little different, like, how could you get the best answers without asking the best questions *first*?"

> How could you get the best answers
> without asking the best questions first?

Brandon looked thoughtful and then asked, "But how can you tell if you're asking the best questions?"

"Now *there's* an important question," Sophie said. She walked to the front of the room. "Do you mind?" she asked, pointing to the white board. I nodded.

"First," she said, "I'm going to draw a kind of map."

With amazing speed that must have come from years of practice, Sophie sketched a big Choice Map on the board. It didn't have all the details but it had the essential elements. I listened as she explained the map to the class in simple age-appropriate language. Everybody agreed that the best questions were on the Learner path and that the ones on the Judger path just made you feel bad. One student volunteered that Judger questions mostly made him mad.

As Sophie and the class discussed the map, Carmen passed me a note that said: "Did you ever notice that when Brandon goes Judger, he goes Judger on other people? And when Becky goes Judger, she goes Judger on herself?" I turned to Carmen, smiled and gave her a thumbs-up. She was really onto something important.

The clock on the wall indicated that we were coming to the end of the school day. I was worried that Sophie wouldn't be able to finish her lesson with the kids. But I needn't have worried, not about someone who'd spent her whole life in the classroom.

"What the Choice Map shows us is a way to find our way inside our own thoughts and feelings," Sophie was saying. "Anything else?"

"It really is like a map then, isn't it," one of the children up close to the board said. "It shows you what directions you could take."

"You can always tell when somebody is being Judger about you," Brandon spoke up in such a loud voice that some of the kids turned and looked at him.

"You sure can," Sophie said, glancing at her watch. "I think we'll have to end right there. Mrs. Shepherd and Mrs. Santiago will take over now. You'll have to think of some really good questions for them."

Someone in the class clapped and then, in unison, all the kids were clapping, giving Sophie an enthusiastic round of applause. Carmen and I dismissed class, and Carmen rushed off to pick up her niece at the high school. I walked Sophie out to the parking lot where we'd left our cars. We were discussing her visit when I heard a voice behind us. We both turned at the same time. Brandon was standing a little behind us, hands in his pockets and looking down at his feet.

"Is it okay? Could I ask a question?"

"You sure can," Sophie said, warmly.

Brandon looked up, beaming with pleasure. He walked over and stood by Sophie. She put her hand on his shoulder and he automatically leaned against her hip, gazing up at her. "Is it really okay to ask questions like you told us in there?" he asked. "That doesn't mean you're stupid?"

"Oh, for goodness sake," Sophie said. "It's just the opposite! It means you're using your own mind." She tapped him gently in the top of his head. "It means you're really getting things working in there, making all that brain machinery work. Maybe sometimes you do have to be careful about who you're asking and *how* you're asking. The important thing is to keep asking lots and lots of questions, especially of yourself, and then patiently watch, and wait, and listen. Sometimes the questions you ask can lead to a kind of treasure, and you never know what that's going to be."

"Really?" Brandon looked up at Sophie, his eyes wide with a sense of wonder and curiosity. "Can I say something?"

"Sure," Sophie said.

"You're like my grandma. I hope you never die like her."

That just about took my breath away. But Sophie smiled, obviously touched by what he'd said. She knelt down a bit and gave him a hug. "Brandon, I'm so glad I met you. You're a fine

CHAPTER 6 : Listening with Learner Ears

young man. I think you're going to work very hard and learn a lot and be a big help to Mrs. Shepherd and Mrs. Santiago. I'll be back to visit you and your class one of these days."

"Okay," Brandon said, looking over at me. "I'll see you next week, Mrs. Shepherd."

"Next week," I said. "Have a great weekend."

He nodded, then turned and raced off to catch the bus.

CHAPTER 7

QUESTIONS OUT OF THE BOX

If we would have new knowledge we must get
a whole world of new questions.
Susanne K. Langer

One afternoon, after our students had left for the day, I remembered a special teaching aid Sophie had used in the sixth grade class. She had called it her Question Box, or QB. It started with a simple cardboard box decorated with colorful paper, with a slot on top like a small ballot box. She'd placed a bright yellow label on the top that said *All Questions Welcome.* With this simple box Sophie taught us so much about mindsets and how they affect virtually everything in our lives. As I shared this memory with Carmen, more and more details came back to mind, giving me new appreciation for what Sophie had taught us about the importance of questions, especially the ones we think with.

The Question Box was always available, sitting on a table by the classroom door. Anytime we wanted to, we could write a question on a slip of paper and stuff it in the box. We didn't have to put our names on the notes either. A couple times a week Sophie drew out one or two of those notes, read them out loud to us, and wrote them on the white board. Then we'd discuss the questions in terms of Judger and Learner mindsets and where that question might take us. Sometimes Sophie or one of us would draw pictures on the board to illustrate how the person with that question might be thinking or feeling.

"Let me give you an example," I told Carmen. "I've never told anyone else. When my parents were upset with me for something I'd done, they often yelled things like: *What's wrong with you? Can't you do anything right?* Or, *you'll always be the dumb one. You'll never make anything of yourself.* Being just a kid, I thought everything they said about me was true, so I really did believe there was something fundamentally wrong with me. I started wondering all the time why I was such a failure at everything. That became my mindset about myself, that I was hopeless and I couldn't ever change. It was just who I was. The fact that I couldn't do anything right was proven nearly every day of my life. There didn't seem to be much I could do about it, either. I'd try really hard, and the harder I tried, the more I messed up. At the time I really believed that those awful opinions about myself were *factual.*"

"I'm so sorry," Carmen said. "That's terrible. Judger mindsets were working overtime, your parents' as well as yours."

"You're not kidding," I said. "I was almost always in bigtime Judger. One day I got up the courage to write a note for the Question Box. I'd thought about doing it for weeks. After I wrote it, I folded it up carefully and slipped it into the box when nobody was looking. Of course, I didn't dare sign it.

"I figured Mrs. Goodwin wouldn't get to my question for at least a week—and maybe never. But guess whose question she pulled out first thing that day, completely at random? I could tell it was mine by the tight little way I had folded it. As she read my note, I held my breath. She wrinkled her forehead, turned away to write my question on the white board, then turned back to us. 'This is the question we'll study today,' she said. And then she read my question aloud so that everyone heard it: *Why am I such a failure at everything?*

"I thought I was going to die. My heart pounded so hard I was sure I was going to have a heart attack or something. But then Dr. Goodwin—Sophie—surprised me. She said, 'A lot of us feel this way sometimes. I know I do.'

"Had I heard her right? Did she actually say *she* sometimes felt like that too? Why would she even admit to such a thing?"

"Well," Carmen said. "She was probably just being honest. I must admit, I've certainly felt that way at times."

Carmen's response stopped me for a second. I am still surprised when other people admit to being Judger on themselves. "As usual," I continued, "Sophie asked us to decide where we'd put a question like that on the Choice Map. A chorus of voices said it should be down there in the Judger pit, stuck in the mud.

"Then, with the kindest, most accepting voice, Sophie said, 'Children, raise your hand if you have *never, ever*, not even once in your whole life, felt like that.' Some of the kids snickered. But not a single hand went up. Everyone had experienced Judger mindset.

"After that, Sophie asked for help drawing a figure on the white board that showed how we might feel asking that question. Someone suggested drawing a big frown on the figure's face. Another kid suggested the figure be all hunched over with its head hanging down."

I paused, remembering an entry from Sophie's journal.

"Sophie says we all have an *inner critic* that frequently throws mean comments our way," I told Carmen. "That's Judger mindset, of course. And it almost always hurts. But she wrote in her journal that this is only a problem when we *believe* that the inner critic is telling the truth. Through that exercise with her Question Box I learned that I have a choice about what I believe. There is a difference between facts and beliefs. Beliefs are just beliefs. They're not facts. Sophie taught us to challenge and question our beliefs to see if they're really working for us. After we've examined our beliefs, we can choose to change them and one way to do that is by changing the questions we ask ourselves."

"Interesting," Carmen said. "Can you give me an example?"

"Sure. Let's take my question, *why am I such a failure at everything?* We'd start by thinking of Learner questions instead of Judger ones, like: *Is that really true? What can I learn from that mistake? If I messed this up, does that mean I mess up everything? What's something really good I've done recently? What's one thing I appreciate about myself?* These new questions switched my mindset from Judger to Learner. I started telling myself, 'Okay, I made a mistake. That doesn't mean *I* am a mistake or a failure. What can I learn so I'll do better next time?'

"When I focused on the Learner questions, I no longer felt like every mistake I made was a dead-end that proved what a loser I was. I saw that whatever happened could be the start of a learning process, and that I could change. Also, as I learned the impact of the different mindsets, I became much more careful about my self-talk, that is, what I told myself. Of course I couldn't have articulated most of this at the time, but with what I'm learning from Sophie I can now see how it all worked for me.

"Looking back, I now realize that as I got better at being in Learner mindset, I wasn't so afraid to *be seen* anymore. I started raising my hand and actually participating in class. That seems like a simple change but for me it was huge. I stopped beating myself up for every little thing. I could study without Judger barraging me all the time, telling me I'd never understand anything or that I'd never get it right, or simply how dumb I was. I started to enjoy studying and thinking. I became a real student and started getting good grades—*consistently* getting really good grades. My brain started working in a very different way. And, you know, it really felt good. It still feels good."

"That's so important," Carmen said. "At home I have this quote by Simone Weil from *Waiting for God* pinned up by my desk: '*The joy of learning is as indispensable in study as breathing is in running.*'"

"In Sophie's journal writings," I said, "she says that teachers can't ignore the student's basic esteem needs, nor can they ignore their own. She quotes educational studies and brain research that shows the correlations between self-esteem and our ability to both learn and teach. That's all about mindsets! So much of what we can accomplish in the classroom depends on the mindset of both teacher and student, and self-esteem sure doesn't get nurtured in a Judger climate."

"Ah hah," Carmen said. "That's like Abraham Maslow's *hierarchy of needs,* which we studied in educational psychology.[15] It's the principle that we can't focus our full attention on learning or doing anything that requires complex thought until our basic needs are met. One of our basic needs is a sense of belonging, which comes from feeling valued by people and by ourselves. Until those needs are fairly well fulfilled, it's very difficult to give our full attention to anything else."

I nodded. "Appreciating ourselves and each of our students, no matter what, is the underpinning for creating a Learner climate in our classroom."[16]

Carmen nodded emphatically. "We may not be able to make the whole world safe for our students but at least we can do our best to create a little safety in the classroom while they're at school."

"We need one of those Question Boxes in our own classroom," Carmen exclaimed.

A few days later Carmen surprised us all with a Question Box she had made at home. It was in the shape of a cube, just a foot wide in each dimension, made from a box she'd gotten at the Post Office. She'd collaged the sides with old roadmaps, reminding us that this was about mapping the geography of our minds. She'd even labeled it the way Sophie did: *All Questions Welcome*. It was beautiful. Kids started asking questions about it right away. Soon there were over a dozen anonymous notes in the box. Carmen had the honor of randomly drawing the first one. A hush fell over the room. You would have thought it was a drawing for the lottery.

Carmen read the note, then said: "This is something I hear on the playground a lot." She wrote on the white board in bold red letters: *What's your problem?*

Brandon shouted from across the room: "That's not a question! It's just a putdown. It just means get away from me or I'm going to . . ."

I turned to face him, feeling myself slipping into Judger. "Brandon, please keep your voice down. You don't have to yell. We can hear you just fine." I was ready to threaten him with an X on the Behavior Chart, which was still on the bulletin board. Then I noticed the expression on his face. I was really touched by how earnest he looked.

"Okay," he said, making a noticeable effort to control himself. "I'll talk softer. But what Mrs. Santiago just wrote is not a question. It's just somebody putting me down . . . I mean putting somebody down. That's all it is."

Carmen and I exchanged glances. She asked Brandon, "So, would you tell us what it is . . ."

"Duh," Brandon interrupted. "It's just plain Judger. It's like when you're in that Judger pit yourself and you put somebody else down just because you're feeling like sh...well, you know what I mean, bad. You want to kick someone's butt."

"Okay," Carmen said, drawing out the word, *ohhh-o-kay*! "I wonder how that would look if it was a figure on the Choice Map." She started to hand the dry erase marker to me.

"Let me do it, okay?" Brandon said. He leapt from his seat and held out his hand for the marker.

We watched as Brandon deftly sketched a very expressive stick figure stuck in the muddy Judger pit, complete with an angry scowl, pointing at someone outside the picture. When he was done he drew a bubble over the figure's head and wrote inside, *What's your problem?*

"There," he said, stepping back to admire his work. "That's how it is, like that."

A voice came from the class: "That's like you, Brandon."

Brandon jerked his head around trying to see who'd said that. "Hey," he said. "I'm just drawing it so everybody can see how it feels."

"That's great, Brandon," I interrupted. "Sometimes I feel like that, too. I just noticed, it looks like the guy you drew is yelling at somebody way back there." I pointed toward the back of the room.

Brandon nodded, looking quite pleased with himself. "That's right," he said. "He got himself in that Judger pit but he's trying to put it off onto somebody else. That's how it works."

"You're very perceptive," Carmen said. "I really like your drawing. It shows how easy it is to feel that way, getting stuck in Judger and blaming other people for whatever happened to us or for how we feel."

"Yeah," Brandon said. "Can I sit down now?"

The whole class was quiet for the longest time. I was thinking how I'd reactively gone Judger when Brandon first bellowed out, *That's not a question!* I had managed to pause just long enough to switch to Learner mindset. I couldn't help but think that we might have missed that wonderful interaction with Brandon had I taken the Judger path.

After class, Carmen and I talked about what had happened and agreed that we'd never seen Brandon quite so engaged. What a breakthrough for him! Besides, we were excited to learn that he had an artistic flair. That figure he'd drawn with just a few simple lines had been surprisingly expressive and had gotten his message across exceedingly well.

"I think we've got a winner with our Question Box," I said.

We decided to take fifteen minutes a couple times a week to explore mindsets with our new Question Box. How might it affect the climate in our classroom, maybe even encouraging our kids to become more self-aware, more accepting and appreciative, more open and thoughtful?

Brandon wasn't the only one who had a breakthrough that day. The Question Box exercise had helped me understand more deeply how important it was to step back and be self-observing, to check out my mindset and create an opportunity to change it. If I expressed myself from Learner mindset more often, how would that affect the weather in our classroom? And how would that affect my kids? By observing my thoughts and feelings in real time, I'd been more responsive to Brandon, more respectful, and more open to the possibility that he really did have something to contribute. He had felt acknowledged. I had listened with Learner ears, as Jared would have said, and it turned out great.

Brandon still had a lot to learn about self-control. Of that I was sure. I didn't know much about his life outside of school or what might have made him the way he showed up in class. What I did know was that going Judger on him had nearly always escalated the problem. My shifting to Learner had given me a new perspective about him as well as about my own abilities as a teacher.

While I'd done okay that day switching from Judger to Learner, I still wondered, did Sophie have some simple, reliable way to make that switch, maybe a tool to help us become better *weather makers* in the classroom? She had already taught me how to recognize body sensations and other signals that could alert me about which mindset, Judger or Learner, was in charge at that moment. That had been a big help. I was hoping she had a next step for me to learn.

I called Sophie as soon as I got home and told her about Brandon's breakthrough—and my own! I also described what I had observed about shifting my mindsets. "I definitely get the principle," I said, "but when it comes to switching when there's lots of pressure I'm not very confident of my own abilities. Too often I've jumped into Judger before I know it."

"And then there's thunder and lightning on the horizon," Sophie said. "Children these days are living with enough storms in their lives. Sadly, I sometimes think that creating classrooms where they can feel safe may be our first priority in education. And that's no small thing. Listen, I've got an idea, Emma. How about you and your friend Carmen coming over to my place on Saturday for a conversation about how to intentionally switch mindsets? I think of it as *the mechanism for managing mindsets.* You'll both find it's as easy as ABCD."

"I'll call Carmen right away," I said, certain she wouldn't turn down an offer like that.

CHAPTER 8

EASY AS ABCD

There is a crucial difference between being caught up
in a feeling and becoming aware that you are
being swept away by it. Socrates' injunction,
'know thyself,' speaks to this keystone
of emotional intelligence: awareness of one's
own feelings as they occur.

Daniel Goleman

As with my first visit, I rang Sophie's bell at the street entrance
and was quickly buzzed into the vestibule. Sophie met me at the
elevator, greeting me enthusiastically. Carmen was driving up
with her husband who was going to drop her off for our meeting. They'd phoned to say they'd be a few minutes late.

Sophie's living room was cluttered with archive boxes. "I'm
moving some things over here from my office at the university,"
she apologized. "I'd hoped to have all this sorted out before you
arrived."

She led me into her small, beautifully appointed kitchen, the kind that instantly tells you the owner loves to cook. A rack over the range showed off a collection of excellent cookware, their shiny copper bottoms reflecting a warm light. I settled into the comfortable breakfast nook while she prepared tea.

"I love entertaining friends in the kitchen," she said. "That way we can talk while I keep an eye on my oven. I hope you don't mind."

"I don't mind at all," I said. "This makes me feel quite at home."

I turned to look out the bay window in the breakfast nook, initially curious about the gardens and lawns below but instead my attention was captured by the luminous stained glass artwork hanging in the window. It wasn't a large piece, approximately the dimensions of a 3-ring binder and beautifully crafted. At the center was the multi-hued question mark I'd come to regard as Sophie's trademark. It had to be the same stained glass artwork I'd seen as a child in Sophie's class. That glowing question mark transported me back once again to the experience of being in her classroom.

The tinkling of china as Sophie placed her beautiful, hand-painted tea service on the table brought me back to the present. She sat down across from me and pointed at the stained glass question mark. "I hung it there yesterday just to inspire you," she said.

"Oh, it does bring back some wonderful memories," I said. "But mostly it reminds me of how much I need to learn so I can be the kind of teacher you were for me."

"What I have to offer is not so much about teaching subject matter," Sophie said. "It's about the *intangibles* of teaching. I believe that's the part that was so transformational for you as a child. You've probably heard that old saying, 'students don't care how much you know until they know how much you care.'

Subject matter is *what* you teach. I'm referring more to *how* you teach, and most of all, to *who you're being* when you teach."

"Carmen and I are starting to experience that with our kids," I said. "And it really came home for both of us when you visited our class. Even the children recognized it. In the blink of an eye you took command of our class like you'd known those kids all their lives. They really perked up. It was like you brought the sun out. And they loved you. You're a very special person, Sophie."

Sophie chuckled. "Thank you for telling me that. But let me assure you that the way I teach is not unique. Everyone develops his or her own way of applying these mindset skills and you will too. What I offer brings each teacher closer to their own strengths and ways of teaching, even with a set curriculum. I believe that one day all these mindset skills will be seen as fundamental for academic success, and for success in life, too."

A gentle three-tone bell chimed in the living room, announcing Carmen's arrival. When Sophie brought her into the cozy kitchen, Carmen immediately commented on the stained glass question mark and the Einstein quote and wanted to know all about it. I told her the story about the first time I'd first seen it, the day I walked into Sophie's classroom. But soon Sophie turned the conversation back to teaching.

"With many students, especially those in K through 12," she said, "the quality of connection between student and teacher, and between student and student, can be at least as important as the subject matter. The younger the child, the more important is this sense of connectedness. Without that connectedness, you might be presenting exactly the subject matter you want students to learn but it's like you're talking to them on a cell phone with a weak signal. They just won't be able to take in anything very well.

"I hasten to add that I'm not talking about being your students' best friend or running a popularity contest. In fact, I discourage that. It's my experience that when teachers worry too much about approval from their students, it can actually get in the way of the kind of connectedness we're talking about here. It's the mindset of the teacher that makes the most difference. And that's where the Choice Map helps you on a moment-to-moment basis as you lead your class.

"Let me tell you a story about a man I met through my consulting practice. This man—let's call him Mr. X—came from an academic family. Both his parents were college professors but he wanted to work with younger children when, as he put it, the child first discovers the magic of 'intentional learning,' when they seek out knowledge because it satisfies something deep within them.

"He taught for a while at an exclusive private school with a strong university track but he got bored. Then he taught at a large, inner-city school but that was not an ideal fit for him, either. At least not at first. He became quite disillusioned. I was working as a consultant at the school and I'll always remember my first meeting with him: 'These kids are just plain crazy,' he'd said. 'They have no interest in learning. They'll never make anything of their lives.'

"I asked him to consider joining a group I'd formed with some other teachers at the school. The core of our work together was how our mindsets influence teaching, learning, and change. We used the Choice Map to guide us to make conscious choices about the mindset we brought to the classroom and its impact on each student."

Sophie sipped her tea thoughtfully. "Soon Mr. X had a breakthrough concerning his responsibility for creating the *weather* in the classroom. As he put it, 'Every child brings his or her own mindset to the classroom, which also impacts that weather. Even so, the teacher's response to what happens will either calm a threatening storm or stir it up into a hurricane.'

"He became highly skillful at observing his own mindset. His Judger mindset was still often triggered by his students' behavior. After all, he had some very resistant and even combative students, who'd grown up in a neighborhood where basic necessities like personal safety were a constant struggle. Every day he spent most of his time putting out brushfires instead of teaching, and this challenged his view of what it meant to be a teacher. How could you call yourself a teacher if you could hardly find time to teach the actual subject matter?

"Our teachers' group kept journals and often shared what we'd written. Mr. X kept a detailed log of everything that touched off his Judger mindset—anger at the school administration for not providing better resources and facilities, anger at students for disruptive behavior, anger at society for not doing better by the kids, and so on. Fortunately he was also very honest with himself. He began to take responsibility for how many of his negative assumptions, especially about his kids, were contributing to the bad weather he brought to the classroom.

"One day he read us a passage from his journal. I still remember how he began: 'Each day I bring a rumbling of thunder to my classroom, creating weather that sends many of my students running for cover.' What's more, he didn't leave that Judger mindset at school. It had begun running his life, every part of it. This realization was his turning point. He said: 'Good teaching starts with your own mindset, with your ability to connect with your students and awaken their curiosity.'"

"Exactly," I said, feeling myself getting a little shrill. "I understand the principles of the Choice Map pretty well, I think. I've even gotten better at recognizing when I've gone Judger.

But certain situations still send me headlong into Judger before I can even think. When that happens, how do I recover enough to change my mindset?"

"I agree," Carmen added. "And how do we do it *quickly*, before we've sent a thunderbolt through the classroom, or gotten ourselves bogged down in that pit?"

"That's where the Switching Lane comes in," Sophie said. "I know we've talked about it before, but now it's time to get more specific and practical about it. It's more than just a term. The Switching lane is a practical mechanism for managing our mindsets. Or, if you prefer, a mental tool for self-regulation and self-management.[17] I also like to think of it as the sweet spot of change." She reached for a Choice Map she had nearby and propped it up on the windowsill. "Let's focus on that little sign near the Switching Lane, *Ask Learner Questions to Avoid Judger Pit*..."

"... and to avoid creating a storm in the classroom," Carmen added.

The Switching Lane is a practical mechanism for managing our mindsets.

All three of us laughed. "Especially that," I said.

"Mr. X began examining the kinds of questions he was asking himself, starting with that first one of his: *How could anybody reach students like these?* He realized that this question was based on Judger assumptions. It absolved him of any responsibility and blamed everything on his students. I asked him to restate this as a Learner question.

"He came up with: *How are my assumptions about the kids getting in the way of their learning? How can I get better at reaching my students? What can I do to change the weather?* And of course there are those Learner questions on the Choice Map:

What's possible? What are they thinking, feeling, or needing? And then he added: *What can I learn?*

"It's always amazing to me," Sophie continued, "that when somebody switches their questions from Judger mindset to Learner mindset, I can practically see the change occurring before my very eyes. Their questions, their curiosity, transforms them. You can see it in their faces and body language. The tone of their voices changes, becoming more relaxed and open. I think they even listen better."

"I've noticed that," I said. "When I'm in Learner the kids participate more openly and enthusiastically."

Sophie held up her index finger. "Good point," she said. "When true curiosity is awakened in this way, we literally do become more present, more engaged. We relate to each other and to our subject matter in a very different way. It opens the inner doors of learning."

"That's what excites me so much about learning, and I love bringing that experience to my students," Carmen said. "What you've given us with these tools, Sophie, makes the experience of learning and teaching so much more accessible—and do-able!"

"I'd love to be a better weatherman. Or, should I say weather *person*," I said, all of us laughing at my metaphor. "But it isn't just about predicting the weather. As Mark Twain famously quoted his friend Charles Dudley Warner, 'Everybody talks about the weather but nobody does anything about it.' I want to be the person who does something about the weather in my own classroom. I want to learn how to detect the earliest signals, when changing the weather is easiest. I want to be the wizard who sees the gathering storm and changes it to a sunny day."

Carmen and Sophie both laughed out loud.

"I can't promise magic," Sophie said. "However, what I do know is that your own curiosity can be your fast track from

Judger to Learner, the inner compass that helps you step onto the Switching Lane. But bear in mind the unbelievable pressures, not to mention lack of respect that so many teachers experience. There are endless influences that can trigger a Judger mindset. So I am not saying that all this is a panacea. But it certainly can help to know whether your Judger mindset was triggered from something outside you, such as a child acting out, or from inside you, such as when you're feeling bad about yourself or challenged by something in your private life.

> Curiosity is your fast track from Judger to Learner.

"I showed Mr. X something I call the *ABCD Choice Process*. The letters stand for: *Aware, Breathe, Curiosity,* and *Decide.* The instant you're aware of tensing up, recognize that your body is telling you that you're going Judger."

"That's the *weathervane,*" Carmen suggested.

Sophie chuckled. "Yes, the weathervane. Even the tiniest neuromuscular responses help you identify what mindset you're in."

She then proceeded to explain more about the ABCD Choice Process:

"**Aware.** Ask yourself, *Am I in Judger?*

"When Mr. X heard this, he said, 'You know, I pride myself on being a critical thinker. But critical thinking means critical in a positive sense, not to be confused with Judger criticism. In fact, going Judger actually interferes with good critical thinking. I know that when I'm under pressure I slip into Judger. I stop looking at the big picture, at the facts in front of me, at what I've got to work with, I focus instead on what's wrong. When I'm in Judger mindset I can't listen openly to my students. If I believe they're not being respectful toward me, I start getting even more Judger. I label them as wrong or hopeless, and that's when

I get stuck.' Mr. X's awareness is the kind of mindfulness we associate with this first segment of the ABCD process—being *aware*. The big challenge is to be a neutral, moment-to-moment observer of your own thoughts and feelings, to not be judgmental about Judger, your own or anyone else's. What's next is . . .

"**Breathe!** Breathing, full breathing, helps restore equanimity; it helps calm down our stress responses and quell a storm that could be building up inside. So pause, step back, and look at the present situation more objectively. When I described this to Mr. X, he took a deep breath, exhaled, and admitted that, in spite of all his training as an educator, he was being anything but objective. His preconceptions of what teaching *should* be were challenged by real life and the very children he most wanted to reach. It was his Judger mindset that was interfering much more than the children. The next step in the process is . . .

"**Curiosity.** From a calmer and more neutral position, of even allowing ourselves to be comfortable with *not knowing*, we can now ask genuine questions like, what's actually happening here? What assumptions am I making? What's really going on with my students? How can I feel more *connectedness* with them? When I asked those core questions, Mr. X was quick to respond. He told me, 'I'm flooded with questions about my responsibility for reaching these kids, for creating the sort of connectedness that I know makes the magic of learning possible.' That, of course, is the essence of curiosity—being full of open-minded questions.[18]

"**Decide.** Okay, what do I choose to do? We've got to decide—make a decision—before we can take action. Remember, Mr. X was on the verge of changing his career path even though he was still deeply committed to education. I told him about a certain kind of question my brother Joseph taught me long ago: *What don't I know? What am I missing?* Mr. X asked how does

ABCD Choice Process

A Aware.

Am I in Judger? Or, Is this working?

B Breathe!

Do I need to step back, pause, and gain perspective?

C Curiosity.

What would be best for me and for others?

What Switching questions should I ask myself?

D Decide.

Now, what do I choose to do?

one go about looking for questions he doesn't even know he's missing? I recalled a line from one of my favorite poets, Rainer Maria Rilke: . . . try to love the questions themselves . . .

"I'm dying to hear the rest of the story," I said. "Did Mr. X stay in education? What did he decide?"

Sophie sipped her tea and looked at me over the rim of her cup. "Mr. X found that in order to make a decision and take action, he had to ask a lot of questions he'd never thought of before. His approach to teaching changed dramatically as he learned to use the ABCD Choice Process and the Switching Lane. Through the simple technique of switching to Learner he dramatically changed his relationship with his students. His new questions opened his mind to considering what he needed to do to engage them, what he needed to learn to understand their needs, and what would work with them. His connectedness with them grew. He sensed that the kids were really listening to him for the first time, because he was listening to *them*. They were much more engaged—not because they were afraid of being punished or getting a bad grade, though I can assure you their grades did improve significantly."

"That's an inspiring story," Carmen said.

Sophie smiled and nodded. "Mr. X changed and his students changed. The weather in his classroom changed. Soon he noticed a new sense of safety, respect and belonging. Children began accomplishing new things—learning and achieving in ways that surprised even them. The world outside the classroom didn't change, but Mr. X had created his own island of learning. Now the children could take risks and experience a sense of safety and respect where intentional learning became possible. Mr. X became an excellent teacher. But he also changed the direction of his career."

"He quit teaching?" Carmen exclaimed. "But why? He must have been such an asset to his school and the kids . . ."

"I didn't say he quit *education*," Sophie added hastily. "Today he's an educational leader who is gifted at bringing around schools in transition."

"He sounds a lot like Dr. Marshall, our principal at Greenfield," I mused.

"Is that so," Sophie said with a twinkle in her eye. "Imagine that! You can't possibly mean the same man who suggested you come and speak with me?"

My jaw dropped. I think I even let out a squeal.

"I wasn't sure I should tell you," Sophie said. "But he gave his okay. How delightful that you're now at the same school."

She reached into a pocket in the folds of her dress and drew out a hanky, dabbing lightly at her eyes.

Before we left that day, Sophie reminded us, "Using the Switching Lane to shift from Judger to Learner is as simple as ABCD! Practice it whenever you become aware of those early Judger signals. And think of every challenge as an opportunity to practice your ABCD's. The goal is to become more resilient as a Learner, just as if you were practicing your golf swing, or tennis serve, or yoga posture, or anything else. In no time, it'll become second nature to you. Then, when you're challenged by something big, you'll have your skills honed and be ready and able to take the Switching Lane. You won't feel like you have to go into survival mode where your only options are fighting, running, or freezing up. You'll be able to get to Learner, where you'll always be most resourceful and strategic, and able to see the most options."

Soon after this, we said our goodbyes. Outside we found Carmen's husband parked at the curb, waiting to pick her up. I was feeling a bit pressed for time since I'd planned to do some shopping and pick up the dry cleaning before meeting Jared for dinner. When I got to the parking lot where I'd left my car, I discovered an old pickup truck had blocked me in. The back of it was filled with sacks of compost and some garden tools, but the driver himself was nowhere in sight. How annoying! Didn't this guy stop to consider that he could be inconveniencing someone? What if I'd had an emergency?

I unlocked my car and yanked the door open. I sat down on the edge of the seat and began rehearsing an angry speech for when that guy showed up. I was steaming and my whole body had tensed up.

Suddenly I stopped myself. *Judger signals! Go to the Switching Lane. Simple as ABCD!* What had Sophie said? Use every Judger moment as an opportunity to practice switching. Okay, I thought, here we go. I glanced over my tense shoulder at the truck. *A. Aware,* I whispered to myself. Am I in Judger? No doubt about that. I was ready to strangle that driver. *B: Breathe!* I slid back the seat, stretched out and took a deep, relaxing breath. Ahhh! That felt better. My back muscles softened and a smile slowly crept over my face. What's the big deal? That truck driver would probably be along any minute. *C. Curiosity.* Was there a real emergency that required the driver to leave his vehicle? How else could I think about this? Could I maneuver around the truck, if it came to that?

Questions tumbled around in my mind. Would the world come to an end if I didn't pick up the dry cleaning tonight? I was actually having fun with this. I thought about each question and imagined where it might take me if I followed through with it.

D. Decide. What *would* I actually do about this? Was this problem worth getting all wound up about? Who might I call on my cell phone if the driver didn't show up? Should I walk around and see if I could find him?

At that moment I heard a cheerful voice calling to me from across the parking lot.

"Hello! I'm so sorry." An attractive older woman with dirt-smudged jeans and a green apron jogged over to me. I recognized her as the neighbor who'd brought flowers to Sophie during my previous visit.

"You're Sophie's friend," the woman said, extending her hand. "I'm Charlotte, her neighbor."

"Of course," I said. "I remember. Your flowers were beautiful, by the way."

She leaned close and asked quietly: "How is she doing?"

"She's fine," I said. Was that a tone of trepidation in Charlotte's voice?

"That's good to hear. She's always been so active."

"Yes," I replied automatically. Did I dare probe Charlotte any further? What did she mean by Sophie always being so active? She was still very active. Wouldn't she have told me if something were wrong?

"I apologize for blocking you in. I hope it wasn't long."

"No. It's fine," I said. "It was just a couple minutes."

"Nevertheless, it was thoughtless of me. I hope you weren't inconvenienced."

Charlotte said goodbye, climbed into her truck and drove off. I was feeling a bit shaky as I put the key in the ignition and started my car. Maybe I should go back upstairs and ask Sophie if everything was okay. Was she ill? Was there a family crisis? I remembered the boxes stacked up in her living room. She'd said they had something to do with the university. I would call Sophie the minute I got home. Or maybe I shouldn't pry. Probably she would have told me if she'd wanted me to know anything.

I drove out of the parking lot remembering a few references Sophie had made about her health. Was I making mountains out of molehills? My dear friend seemed as healthy as ever. Maybe Dr. Marshall knew something. I'd ask him about Sophie on Monday. Meanwhile I soothed myself with reminders that I didn't really have sufficient information to justify my worry. I turned my attention to dinner and how much I was looking forward to a leisurely evening with my husband.

CHAPTER 9

BECOMING A RESILIENT LEARNER

We keep moving forward, opening new doors,
and doing new things, because we're curious
and curiosity keeps leading us down new paths.

Walt Disney

I glanced at my watch as I pulled into the restaurant parking lot, noting that I was about 20 minutes late. Late or not, I took a minute to glance in the car mirror and fix my hair. Inside the restaurant, the maître d' escorted me to our table. Jared gave me a peremptory hug and kiss, and I sat down. I didn't have to be a mind reader to tell he wasn't in a great mood. I immediately assumed it was because I was a little late, then reminded myself that there was a difference between assumptions and facts. Still, I was annoyed that Jared might be irritated about my tardiness.

"Sorry for being late," I said.

"It's okay," he said. "It's not a big deal. Really."

Not a big deal. Really. Jared never said that except when just the opposite was true. I was tensing up, putting one foot on that slippery slope of the Judger path. Nobody can push our buttons like the people we love! I'd just come from Sophie's, where I was honing my skills for taking the Switching Lane and here I was, squarely on the Judger path again. Wanting to enjoy my time with Jared, and remembering my ABCDs, I leaned back in my chair and took a deep calming breath. Right away, I felt a little better. It was easier now to get curious and shift my attention to Jared.

"You look exhausted and stressed," I said. "What's going on?"

"I shouldn't have gotten upset about your being late," Jared said. "First I went Judger on you. But then I went Judger on myself. I started wondering if I'd made a stupid mistake. Maybe I'd gotten the day wrong, or had the wrong restaurant." He reached across the table for my hand. "With all the pressure at work, I've been a little on edge lately. Plus, I hate waiting alone in a restaurant. Everyone thinks I've been stood up."

"You don't really think that, do you," I said, trying to hide my astonishment.

Jared gave me a lopsided grin. "Well, it did happen to me once—when I was nineteen. I was supposed to meet my date for dinner but I got the wrong restaurant. That was the end of that!"

"Oh, how awful for you," I said with exaggerated sympathy, knowing he was joking—well, half-joking at least.

The waiter appeared and took our orders. As soon as he left Jared asked, "Would it be okay if I talked about work?"

We had a standing agreement to not talk shop over dinner unless we badly needed to get something off our chests. I was a bit hesitant to agree but was also sure that Sophie's ABCD technique would help if I felt myself getting upset about Jared's problems at work. "That's fine," I told him. "It must be something important."

"Do you recall the guy from marketing I told you about?"

"Mickey Stonewell," I said, proud of myself for remembering. "Sarcastic. Off-color jokes. He thinks he's funny? That one?"

Jared nodded. "I always dread my meetings with him. But today I started doing what we talked about—you know, listening with Learner ears, not automatically reacting, and going Judger on him. It wasn't easy, but I was mostly able to stay focused on the business at hand rather than getting sidetracked by how I usually react to his garbage.

"Mickey can be really offensive. He thinks he's a comedian and I always feel pressured to laugh, you know, just to pacify him. At the very least, it's a big waste of energy when you're up against a deadline. I start thinking, *Man, do you know how stupid you sound?* In any case, today I stayed as neutral as I could and used my Learner ears. I tried to ask positive questions, you know, ones that might keep us focused on the project, and help me vet the information I actually needed from him."

"And he was okay with that?" I asked.

"If anything, he seemed to relax, and stopped playing the fool. That was the first time in months that I left a conversation with him without feeling annoyed. A while later he called me on the phone and asked if I'd meet him for coffee. We went over to Starbucks. He confided that he was *on probation* with two important people in his life, Esther Laufenberg, our boss, and also..."

"Let me guess," I interjected. "His wife."

"Exactly." Jared chuckled. "He and his wife have two kids. I'm sure he loves them very much. And when it comes right down to it, he's good at the nuts and bolts of his job. The trouble comes when he starts clowning around and gets sarcastic. He is so oblivious about how he affects people around him.

That conversation showed me how helpful Sophie's lessons can be in our personal lives and not just at work."

I nodded. "So, he wanted your advice?"

Jared nodded. "I made a rough sketch of the Choice Map on a napkin, and he remembered it from the one hanging in my office. I suggested ways he might use the map to look at some of his assumptions about his wife and Mrs. Laufenberg and why they might be upset with him."

"That was daring of you," I said. "What happened next?"

"Well, he got sarcastic at first. Then I made sure I was in Learner and calmly told him that I believe his sarcasm was what gets him in trouble. Most people perceive it as hostile. Even if he was intending to be funny, it pushed other people's Judger buttons, including mine, thwarting any possibility for open and constructive conversation."

"That must have gone over big," I kidded.

Jared nodded. "You got that right. He stormed out, muttering how nobody has a sense of humor anymore. I figured I'd really blown it, he was so mad. But a little while later he came back. You can imagine how surprised I was. I didn't know what to expect."

"I don't see any black eyes," I said.

"He apologized and wanted to know more about what I'd been saying. I ended up giving him some homework."

"Homework?"

"Yes. When we got back to the office I scanned a copy of the Choice Map for him and went over some Learner questions he might ask himself instead of *joking around*."

"Joking around?"

"Yeah, that's what he calls that sarcasm of his. The notion that other people could find it offensive was startling to him. We looked at the Choice Map together and I asked him what kind of impact he wants to have on the people in his life. Did he want to bring them into Learner territory or down to the Judger pit? Did he want collaboration or conflict? I could tell he was struggling with this, holding back from throwing some smart-alecky response at me. But he didn't. He took a deep breath and exhaled like a winded horse! And then he started nodding. He really got it!"

"That's great work, Jared!"

"The problem is, now he thinks we're pals. He asked if I'd write him a letter of support so they won't fire him. I'm not sure I can honestly do that. And I sure don't want to be his marriage counselor..."

"You can refuse to write that letter, can't you? Besides you wouldn't do anything like that without a lot more information."

Jared got a big grin on his face. "Does that mean you don't think I should be his marriage counselor?"

I reached across the table and squeezed his hand. "That's right. I'm the only one who gets you for that," I said. "Nobody else."

He stared at me for a second or two and then chuckled wickedly. "Okay. I'd like to make an appointment right away."

"Sure," I said. "That is, if you can fit me into your busy schedule."

"Well, I *was* planning on counting my green socks tonight."

"That shouldn't take long," I said. "I happen to know you don't have any green socks."

"Hunh," he said. "How propitious!"

Before I could answer, the waiter stepped in with our salad. "I'm sorry for interrupting," he said. "You two seem deeply involved."

"Very deep stuff," Jared said. "She claims I don't have any green socks."

The waiter looked back and forth between Jared and me, appearing a bit nonplussed. Then he noticed our smiles and quipped, "You're clearly a man of good taste."

All three of us laughed and the waiter proceeded to toss our salad.

CHAPTER 10

QUESTIONING ASSUMPTIONS

Your assumptions are your windows on the world.
Scrub them off every once in a while,
or the light won't come in.
Isaac Asimov

With things going so much better for me at school, I looked forward to getting to the classroom every morning, even on Mondays. But I worried about Becky. I couldn't understand why I still wasn't reaching her, even with all I'd been learning. What was I doing wrong? Why couldn't I get through to her?

I decided to write about my problems with Becky in the journal Sophie had given me. But as I opened it up, I found myself getting tense and feeling resistant. Did I have some Judger lurking around, I wondered. What was my body trying to signal to me? Maybe I could use a reflection exercise to help me figure it out. I wrote down the first questions that popped into my mind:

What am I missing? What makes Becky get mad and withdraw every time I try to talk with her? Am I just no good at reaching underachievers? What's wrong with me that I can't figure this out? What would Sophie do with Becky?

Then I got an idea that at first seemed a little nutty. Maybe I could use this journal writing to have an imaginary conversation with Becky. I'd tell her what was really on my mind and ask her questions I never could if we were talking for real. This is what I wrote:

My Conversation with Becky

Me: (To Becky) What is it about you? You can be so exasperating! I'm sure you're far more thoughtful and intelligent than comes across in your school work. Why can't you just take a little more care? Don't you recognize your own potential? Why do you push me away when I try to point out your gifts to you? Goodness knows, you're not disruptive in class, like others I could mention. Becky the vanishing girl. You're sure good at disappearing, I'll give you that! I just don't get it!!! You act like I'm attacking you just for noticing that you exist. That's when I really go Judger back at you! Maybe I'm just not cut out to be a teacher. Becky, you make me feel so inept—and I hate feeling inept.

Becky: (To me) You really make me mad . . . Don't tell me that stuff about potential, whatever that is. Teachers think they're so smart saying that to kids. I can't do or be potential. Everybody's always saying I don't live up to my potential. Sure, good. That's just more bad news, another way to say I'm failing, that I'm not good enough for you. How can I do something I'm not . . . something that's . . . well . . . not even there? You don't know what I care about. You don't know what I can do. So stop bugging me about doing something that's as invisible to me as . . . I don't know . . . turning into an E.T. or Nemo or some terrible monster. Plus, I don't even believe in stupid monsters like that. You talk to me like I don't matter unless I become exactly what you expect. I just feel so . . .

I stopped right there. I had almost written *I just feel so inept* again! I mean *really again*. This was the same statement I'd just written about *myself*. I went back to writing in my journal:

Me: (To myself) Who am I talking about here—Becky or myself? I realize she's a lot like I was when I was her age. Maybe she was feeling like I did when I wrote that question for Sophie's question box: "Why am I always such a failure?" Didn't the adults around me know that I would if I could? How can you know what you don't know, or do what you don't yet know how to do? From Sophie, I learned the power of starting with what I could do, instead of feeling bad, or going Judger on myself for what I couldn't do. Sophie helped me shift my focus to what was right and worthy about me instead of only what might be wrong or lacking. What are my assumptions about Becky . . . and about what happens between us?

What assumptions am I making?

Suddenly I noticed the clock. I'd gotten so immersed in my journal writing that I'd lost track of time. I'd be late for school if I didn't scoot. I rushed out the door and jumped into my car, munching on a granola bar as I raced across town. When I arrived at our classroom half the kids were already there and Carmen was standing beside my desk with Brandon. He was holding a piece of paper and looking pretty glum. They both turned to me as I walked through the door.

Carmen told me that Brandon had removed the Behavior Chart from the bulletin board. He had said, "I hate it. It's stupid and useless." Carmen had admonished him, "You know the teachers' bulletin board is strictly off limits."

To tell the truth, I didn't know exactly what to do. Carmen and I wanted to get rid of the Behavior Chart, too. But Brandon had violated a strict class rule about never touching anything on the teachers' bulletin board.

"Mrs. Santiago is right," I told Brandon sternly. "The teachers' bulletin board is off-limits. Right now I want you to go to your desk and sit down so we can start class on time. Mrs. Santiago and I will have to talk about this."

"Aw, *man!*" Brandon moaned. He turned and went to his seat, managing to *accidentally* bump into several chairs along the way. Before sitting down he muttered, just loud enough for us to hear, "I hate that Behavior Chart."

Carmen whispered to me: "I didn't know quite what to do. *Estar entre la espada y la pared.*"

I looked at her questioningly since I didn't understand Spanish.

"Sorry," she said. "It means being caught on the horns of a dilemma."

I went over to the bulletin board and put the Behavior Chart back up. It was a little crooked, which I guess showed how I really felt about it. Then I had a brilliant idea, something I remembered from sixth grade. Sometimes, when there was a problem that affected the whole class, Sophie would have us make a list of questions about the incident. If someone asked a Judger question, Sophie would convert it to a Learner question, right on the spot. Recently I'd found a more sophisticated version of this exercise in the blue folder Sophie had given me. She called it *Q-Storming*. This was sort of like brainstorming except looking for questions instead of answers.

The exercise started with something that was very real and

immediately important. The best thing about doing it was that it taught us to pause, to step back so we could reflect on ourselves, on what was happening and what we really wanted to happen instead of just automatically reacting and getting all riled up. Sophie's exercise prompted us kids to articulate events in our own lives, giving voice to what we were feeling and experiencing.

The exercise was simple enough. She would collect all our questions and write them on the white board. Each of us would choose one question and write about it for ten minutes. We could write anything we wanted to. I thought we could use this situation with Brandon to find out what the other kids thought about the Behavior Chart. Frankly, my real goal was to get some ideas for changing or improving it.

I talked it over with Carmen and she volunteered to start the class off.

"We need some help," Carmen announced to the children. Brandon bowed his head. I figured he was afraid we were going to talk about him.

"Everybody knows about the Behavior Chart," Carmen asked. "Right?"

A general mumbling of acknowledgement rippled through the class.

"Who can tell us what it's for?" Carmen continued. "Why do we have it?"

Sheila, who sits near the front of the class, raised her hand and Carmen called on her.

"If we didn't have it," Sheila answered, in her usual melo-dramatic tone, "everyone would just act really crazy and stupid and do whatever they wanted. It would be crazy, crazy, crazy in here, and nobody would learn anything." A few kids snickered, amused by Sheila's idiosyncratic exaggerations.

Carmen thanked Sheila and we asked for suggestions about

restating what Sheila said as a Learner question. With some coaching from Carmen and me, we came up with the following, which I wrote on the white board:

"What would stop us from acting crazy and stupid if there were no Behavior Chart?"

Another hand went up. It was Tom, one of our more academically oriented students. Other kids called him a *geek*, which he took as a compliment. As was typical of him, he stood up to speak, body ramrod straight. He spoke in a stiff, pompous tone. "The Behavior Chart provides averages and standards for acting in the classroom." Tom sat down and we took a few moments to convert this to another question:

"What behavior is acceptable in the classroom? What other things in our lives teach us how to act?"

Next, Carmen called on Lisa, who had had her hand raised for a long time. "I don't get it," she said in an argumentative tone. "That chart doesn't tell us anything we don't already know. It's just to punish kids who keep acting up, like Brandon."

"Shut up, Lisa," Brandon said. "You don't know anything."

"Is that the way we talk in class?" I asked Brandon.

"What? Oh. No," he said. "Sorry, Lisa. Okay?"

"Whatever," she said, dismissively.

The whole class became restless, whispering back and forth. Carmen quickly quieted them down. What Lisa had said was true, of course. The Behavior Chart was mainly punitive. It did not actually articulate any standards or guidelines. It wouldn't be easy to translate Lisa's complaint into a Learner question. We discussed it for several minutes. This is what we finally came up with: *How does threatening punishment stop us from acting up?*

Brandon's hand shot up and Carmen pointed to him. "That chart is just plain Judger. That's all. Judger, Judger, Judger! It just makes everybody feel bad."

"It makes you feel bad because you *are* bad," Lisa said. "That's what!"

Brandon slouched down in his chair and set his jaw, doing his best to keep his mouth shut and hold in his feelings. "That's not true," he said. "Don't call me that."

"Okay," Carmen said. "Brandon feels the Behavior Chart is all Judger. How could we let someone know their behavior is unacceptable without going Judger on them?"

"I know what we do at home," Lisa offered. "When we act up Mom says, 'Are you going to stop yourself or do you need me to help you stop?'"

"Yeah, and then she gives you a time out if you don't stop," Lisa's friend Karen added. "Then you have to just sit there and think about it."

"Okay," I said. "Let's write that down: 'Are you going to stop yourself or do you need help to stop?'"

"Also, my dad warns us if he's getting mad or something. I mean, sometimes that happens," Karen added. "He says, *you're making me real angry here!* And if he starts counting, you know you'd better shape up or something bad is going to happen."

Carmen converted what Karen said to a question and wrote it down: "How can we warn people when we're feeling mad or angry?"

We continued with this process and in short order we had a good list of questions relating to the Behavior Chart. Now each child would choose one of them to write about. Within a few seconds everyone was busy writing. Only two children needed a bit of encouragement; then they, too, were bending over their desks, writing enthusiastically. After ten minutes, Carmen and I began collecting their papers. We thanked our students for their help and explained that we would read their work and talk about it again in a few days.

During the lunch break, Carmen and I could hardly wait to read what the children had written. We gathered their papers into a folder and took them out to our favorite lunch spot at the back of the playground. We hoped that the kids' comments would help us better understand the effect of the Behavior Chart—and even help us come up with ideas about what to do instead. We spent the next half-hour reading random selections of our students' work. We soon came up with some questions for ourselves that could help us figure out alternatives to the Behavior Chart:

- How can I stay in Learner while correcting or disciplining a student?

- What can I do so that a student *learns* from his or her behavior and isn't just punished for it?

- What assumptions am I making about this child and his or her behavior?

- How can I teach "behavioral consequences" while encouraging Learner mindset?

- How can I help this student take responsibility for his or her behavior and also develop more *internal controls?*

Before we got any further, we were distracted by a disturbance on the other side of the playground. In an area under the big oak tree, where the children often gathered to talk with their friends, I noticed Brandon standing next to Becky. She was reaching out, trying to grab something away from him. Even from far away I could tell the conflict was escalating. Carmen gathered up our papers while I sprinted across the playground.

"Give me that," Becky screamed at Brandon. "That's *mine*, it's my private stuff!"

"That's stupid," Brandon said. "Everybody should see these."

They were fighting about a few photographs that Brandon was holding in his hand.

"Brandon," I reprimanded. "What's going on here?"

"Never mind," Becky said, looking like she'd burst into tears. "Just please go away."

"Give them back to her," I told Brandon.

He looked at me with a puzzled expression. "No. They belong to me."

"Don't look at them," Becky begged me. "Please don't."

Brandon turned to Becky and said. "You are so good. Everyone should see how good you are. You're being really stupid."

"You already told me that," Becky said. "So I'm stupid, okay? Now are you satisfied?"

"Oh, man, you are so hopeless."

Of course, I was dying to see the pictures but wanted to respect Becky's privacy. At that instant, Brandon jumped in front of me and thrust the pictures in my face, fanned out so I could see them clearly. Between the sudden surprise of his movement and my own curiosity I couldn't help but look at them. They were photos of a skateboarder in a graceful, almost unbelievable movement. In spite of her helmet and other safety equipment, there was no doubt in my mind who it was: Becky. She was high in the air, having just launched off a ramp at the skateboard park. Becky was flying, like the most graceful, beautiful bird you could ever imagine and she had a smile of intense concentration and pleasure on her face.

"Becky! This is absolutely beautiful," I said, tears coming to my eyes. No wonder Brandon wanted other people to see the pictures. "You're like a dancer, flying so effortlessly through the air like that."

Becky stood back, hands on her hips and a belligerent look on her face.

"What's going on?" Carmen had jogged up beside me. In that instant Becky swung her backpack at Brandon, grabbed the photos from his hand and sprinted across the playground. Brandon started to go after her but I stopped him.

"Let her be," I told him.

"She's hopeless," he said, turning to me. "She got all angry because her brother, who's a friend of mine, took those pictures. He gave them to me because she was going to tear them up."

"I don't understand," I said. "These pictures are magnificent. I didn't even know Becky was a skateboarder or any kind of athlete."

"Yeah," Brandon said, "but she can't stand it when anybody says something nice about her if she isn't absolutely perfect. Becky hides all the time. Sometimes I think she doesn't want anybody to know she even exists! She's one of the best skateboarders you'll ever see, a lot better than I'll ever be. She's mad because right after those pictures were taken, she crashed. So? I mean, it's no big deal. She didn't hurt herself or anything. She knows how to crash, but . . ."

"But what?"

"It's like with that Choice Map of yours. Anytime she makes a mistake or somebody tries to tell her anything, she goes all Judger on herself, like a turtle crawling into her shell. I'm just the opposite. When I go Judger I yell at people. I'm like a . . . I don't know . . . like one of those dogs that growls and barks and chases people away. You know what I mean."

Suddenly it all made sense. That day I tried to tell Becky she had potential, she'd crawled into her shell, just as Brandon had described. She'd anticipated disapproval before I said a word. How could a girl who was such a wonderful athlete—who knew how to fly—be so self-critical that she didn't want anybody to see her? How had she ever learned to be so beautifully graceful if she was so, well, *turtle-like*?

"*Que es esto?*" Carmen leaned over, picked something up from the grass and glanced at it.

"She dropped that," Brandon said. He reached out and plucked the picture from Carmen's hand. "I wasn't supposed to show these to anyone."

Carmen looked surprised. "Why not? This is a great picture of her. She's a real artist on that board of hers, like a dancer."

She handed the photo to Brandon and he brushed off a few flecks of dirt. "Becky is going to kill me for showing these to you." He turned and bolted across the playground after Becky.

"You knew about Becky's skateboarding?" I asked Carmen.

"Sure," she said. "My niece goes to that same park. She has soccer practice just a little ways from the skateboarding area. Darlina can skateboard, too, but she's not as good as Becky. Hardly anyone is. That's why they call Becky *The Little Eagle*."

I nodded, feeling a little foolish that I didn't know more about our own kids, and that what I thought I knew about them was actually pretty one-dimensional. Even though we were connecting better lately, I realized that mostly I knew *about* our students, but I didn't really know *them*. What I did know was their grades, school records, their study habits, how much they participated in class, or whether they were troublemakers like Brandon.

The mere thought of how much time it would take to *really* get to know each child threw me into overwhelm considering the many demands and pressures of teaching, most of them not directly related to teaching, that ate away at my time. I could feel myself getting upset and defensive, wanting to argue that it was impossible to connect with *every single* child. I wasn't paid enough to be a social worker, too! That's when I became aware that Judger had taken over.

Taking a breath, I recalled moments with Sophie when I was a child. When she talked to you, it always felt like you were the only person in the world who mattered at that moment. Sometimes that sense of connectedness lasted for only a few seconds. It wasn't like she and I had had long one-on-one conversations or that I thought I was her "pet" or anything. It was just that I deeply knew that I was okay with her. It was the quality of her attention and presence that had made the difference for me. I felt invited and *received* by her.

Then another realization struck me. Sophie wasn't just that way with me; she was like that with all of us. This was what she meant by *being with her students* rather than her way of working being any particular technique. You can't *do* Learner, you can only *be* Learner. You can't do Switching questions like you were thoughtlessly following some abstract formula. You have to actually *want* to be in Learner, that's what made all the difference in her teaching. This was the kind of teacher I wanted to be—one with whom Becky, and students like her, would be willing to risk being *visible*. This was how Sophie made the weather in our classroom. It was always safe and sunny around her, not cloudy or threatening to storm.

> You can't *do* Learner, you can only *be* Learner.

Turning my attention back to Carmen, I smiled and said, "I guess there's a lot more to learn about our students. I'm really looking forward to it."

CHAPTER 11

SURPRISING COLLABORATORS

Good questions help us to become both
curious and uncertain, and this is always the road
that opens us to the surprise of new insight.

Peter Senge

I would learn more about Becky and Brandon in the next few days as Carmen told me about the skateboarding program and other after-school activities at the park.

"Sometimes, after Darlina's soccer practice," Carmen said, "we go across the park and watch the boarders. It's all so well organized, supervised by a male teacher from the high school and a woman from the university. Someone said the woman coach is also one of those brainy people who are just good at everything, athletics as well as intellectual pursuits. They've got a new program started and I noticed that Brandon has been helping the coaches."

121

"Wait a second," I said. "Brandon is a skateboarder?"

"Yes, he's a boarder, but mostly he assists the coaches and the woman who is observing from the university. It's something new. Brandon is really good with the younger kids, you know, helping with their safety equipment and things like that."

"That doesn't sound like the Brandon I know," I said. "Doesn't he scare the younger children? I mean, he can be intimidating."

"He gets pretty loud, yelling at the kids to get their attention. It's very important that they listen to the coaches and stop doing things that could get them hurt. I don't know that much about it, only what I saw when we stopped to watch them the other day. The younger kids look up to Brandon, as far as I can tell."

"I've never seen that side of him," I mused. "You sure it's our Brandon?"

"Oh, I'm sure of it," Carmen said. She added reflectively, "Maybe the problem is that he doesn't know how to feel useful with us, here in the classroom." She was packing her tote bag, getting ready to leave.

"What do you mean?" I must admit I was feeling a little defensive.

Before she could answer me, Carmen's attention turned to a large white envelope which someone had stuck in her tote bag. I recognized the envelope as one I'd tossed into recycling that morning. Carmen slid two photos out of it. "For goodness sake," she said. "They're pictures of my niece Darlina, from that play she was in at the high school. There's a note attached. It says, 'I hope you like these pictures. My brother took them at play practice.' How sweet. Someone must have taken them with their cell phone and printed them out at the computer lab."

Carmen pointed at the stylized sketch of a bird at the bottom of the note.

"Why does that look familiar to me?" I mused.

"It's Becky's trademark. I guess you'd call it her special signature." Carmen smiled as she put the photos carefully into her tote bag. "Becky sometimes draws it at the bottom of her assignments."

A second later Carmen was gone and I was left standing alone by my desk. In the past, when I'd seen Becky's bird drawings on her papers, my only thought had been that she should stop doodling and pay attention to her assignments instead. At this moment, however, two of Sophie's questions popped into my head. Am I in Learner mindset or Judger mindset right now? And am I listening with Learner ears or Judger ears? Frankly my ears got a little hot as I realized yet again how much time I'd spent in Judger about Becky.

Thinking about those doodles and Becky's expert skateboarding suddenly shifted my whole perception of her. Both of those abilities require a high level of skill and organization, suggesting that she had an excellent brain. What I hadn't recognized was how visual and kinesthetic she was and very possibly gifted. Not only that, she certainly showed great *persistence*; Becky had obviously spent *many* long hours skateboarding, perfecting her skills to do what she now did so exquisitely.[19] How could I use Sophie's mindset tools to help Becky channel more of her obvious capabilities into her school work, and into developing the skills that she would need as an adult?

Later that evening, Jared and I both had work to do, so we ate a quick dinner and retreated to our separate offices. I had buried myself in some of Sophie's early journal pages, recorded when she was about my age and just beginning to teach. This entry leapt out from the page:

> It worries me when I think of what I might be missing about
> my students. What assumptions am I making about who they

are and what they can and can't do? What am I assuming about their intelligence and interests and skills? I don't know for sure. Maybe my old questions aren't helping. What questions haven't I asked myself about them before?

The most fulfilling part of teaching has always been when a student suddenly gets what learning is all about, how that changes them, how they begin pursuing learning on their own, just for themselves, for the sheer pleasure and excitement of it. Where are they talented and accomplished outside school that I don't know about as their teacher? Where in their lives do their minds come alive with new discoveries and possibilities, new skills and self-knowledge? How can I bring all of that into the classroom?

Sophie's words struck a definite chord with me. If I didn't know about Becky's athletic talents, what didn't I know about my other students? I began writing earnestly in my own journal, exploring questions I hadn't asked about my own students before. I smiled when I reflected on this and made the obvious correction: What Learner questions haven't I been asking myself about my students? What might I do to discover more about who they are and their innate capacities? What have I been assuming about what it means to be smart, even gifted? How might we make the children's excitement in their outside activities an active part of our weather *inside*, in our school environment? How can I be more effective in reaching my students?

What Learner questions haven't I been asking myself about my students?
What might I do to discover more about who they are
and what innate capacities they have?

I sat and thought about Sophie's words and my own questions for a long time, then reached for the phone and pressed the auto-dialer for Carmen's number. I apologized for calling so late—it was going on nine o'clock—and asked if I could read her an entry from Sophie's journal. After that, I nervously read her what I'd written in my own journal.

"Wow," she said, "this gives me an idea. Parents' Open House is coming up. We need a theme for the bulletin board and table displays. What if we used this idea of Dr. Goodwin's as our focus, you know, highlighting what our kids are doing and learning outside class as well as what they're doing and accomplishing in class? I'm sure it will be eye opening for all of us, parents and kids, as well as for you and me."

That idea led to our hatching the concept for a display of our kids' greatest interests and accomplishments, both in and out of school. We'd have our students collect photos for the bulletin boards and write short compositions about themselves and what these activities meant to them. We'd ask them to come up with other creative ways to showcase what excited them, things they wanted to share about their own accomplishments. We could also have them come up with questions to explore on the internet that would deepen their learning and give them a broader appreciation for their own knowledge and abilities.

I imagined Becky bringing in a picture of her flying in the air on her skateboard, with a written description of how she had developed those skills. Would she even consider such a thing? Maybe if she saw others sharing their experiences she would be inspired to write something about her own—or would it only anger her if I asked her to do it, causing her to withdraw further into her shell, as Brandon had put it. I wondered if there might be a way that he could reach her, given that they seemed to be friends—well, at least when they weren't fighting. The moment this occurred to me I realized something I hadn't thought about during that conflict between them on the playground. What had triggered it? It must have been Brandon's appreciation for Becky's skills and his desire to share those pictures of her skateboarding with other kids. I wondered what might have gone on behind the scenes that I would never know about.

There was so much we didn't know about our kids' lives beyond the walls of the classroom! With that realization, my mind wandered off in a different direction. I started getting curious about what Becky would have had to learn to perform those remarkable athletic feats. How amazing to think of her brain organizing such complex movements while hurtling along the ramps or flying gracefully in the air. It made me dizzy to think about it. The incident with that photo helped me see both Becky and Brandon in a whole new light.

Carmen and I talked for over two hours that night, Q-Storming as we'd done before. She offered a wonderful question: "What would get the kids so engaged that they themselves would spearhead creating the displays for the Open House?" We'd use Q-Storming with them to come up with questions they could explore on the internet, in our school library, or perhaps by interviewing each other. How wonderful it would be to explain to the parents at the Open House how the kids came up with all those questions.

The very next morning we introduced our idea for the Open House project to the class. I took the Choice Map off the bulletin board, pointed to the Learner path and explained that we wanted to give everyone an opportunity to share their accomplishments with other people. It could be something they'd learned and were proud of, either in school or out. It didn't have to be a subject area we were studying, but it would be fine if it were.

The weather in the classroom shifted dramatically that day, though I realized that these changes had been building for some time. Carmen and I were getting increasingly skillful at keeping our-selves in Learner mindset. We also were getting better at recognizing when we were in Judger and switching to Learner. What surprised me, though I guess it shouldn't have, was that the kids were making similar shifts. Sometimes they would stop themselves in the middle of saying something Judger and comment, "I guess that was pretty Judger of me, wasn't it?" Then they'd go on to express themselves in a Learner manner. It was quite apparent to Carmen and me that they were learning by our example since we weren't spending a lot of time directly teaching them about mindset, except for Sophie's one visit and our Question Box exercises. True, the Choice Map was on the bulletin board. Carmen had even placed it lower than the Behavior Chart so that it was closer to the childrens' eye level. Bran-don had cut a big arrow out of red construction paper which he'd had me place next to the Choice Map to bring more attention to it.

Together we were all creating a learning environment that was dynamic and exciting; I could practically envision our stu-dents' minds opening in ways that reminded me of what I'd experienced as a sixth grader with Sophie. And this transition had all been so easy and natural! The changes we were all expe-riencing affirmed why I had become a teacher. I hadn't made a mistake in my choice of profession, as I'd feared not so long ago.

The Open House project was coming together nicely. Many children were bringing in work they'd done at home for the big event. Sometimes they brought computer work or photos, and sometimes they put together actual demonstrations that were presented to the class. For example, Zak had learned how to cre-ate a 3-dimensional image of a chair on an old CADD program (Computer-Aided Design and Drafting) that his dad had given him. Someone else brought in an article, complete with color photos, about something called a *MakerBot*, which would print 3-dimensional, physical objects.

Of course the kids had millions of questions about these projects, especially Zak's CADD drawings and what his friend had discovered about actually "printing" dimensional models. What was the most difficult thing about it? What was the strangest thing about learning how to do these things? What was easiest? What was most surprising? What had each child learned in school that helped him or her put together a project? Carmen was jotting down questions as fast as she could. Later she helped Zak and other children work some of these questions into oral presentations for the big night.

At the center of this activity, Carmen and I began to notice that Brandon and Becky were working collaboratively to keep the overall Open House project focused. Sometimes they were together talking to other kids. At other times I saw Becky helping organize a bulletin board so that it would look good and be easy to read. Occasionally, Brandon stood near the center of the room gesticulating. I couldn't figure out what he was doing until I overheard him explaining how the traffic would flow through the room when visitors arrived and what this meant in terms of moving tables and setting up the room.

One afternoon, a shouting match started in one corner of the room where the bulletin board committee was working. Before Carmen or I could get there to quiet things down, Brandon was in the middle of it. I was certain it was going to explode into a fight. But then I heard Brandon say, "Cool it, you guys."

"Get away," Chad said. "You're not the boss of me."

"I didn't say I was," Brandon said. "I'm just saying . . ."

"Yeah, what are you saying?" Chad stood up abruptly, banging his chair against the wall. He stuck out his chin and clenched his fists.

"I was just saying, what do you guys need here?" Brandon said, holding up his open hands to show Chad that he wasn't going to fight.

"Then buzz off," Chad said, dropping his defensive posture a bit.

"Come on, Chad," one of the other kids said. "Sometimes Brandon's got good ideas."

"He doesn't even know what we're doing," Chad snapped back.

"Didn't say I did," Brandon said. "But like coach Ed Michael says, *'What needs to happen so everyone can win?'* And don't forget what we've been learning with the Choice Map."

What needs to happen so everyone can win?

"Like you're an expert on the Choice Map," Chad said sarcastically.

"Maybe not," Brandon said. "But it's like you guys are all on that Judger path, hassling each other, and getting nowhere."

"I'm not going Judger," one of the other kids argued indignantly.

"Hey, I know how to do Judger better than any of you!" Brandon joked.

"Hunh? What did you just say?" Chad asked. "You're a better Judger than anyone?"

Brandon puffed up his chest with mock pride. "Yup. That's me."

Everyone started laughing and Brandon laughed louder than anyone. "Anyway," he said, "nobody gets anywhere when you're stuck in that Judger pit."

I just stood there with my mouth agape. The kids were working it out, prompted by Brandon's leadership. What was that comment Carmen had made, that maybe Brandon hadn't needed to find a way to feel useful in the classroom? He'd found that place now! Amazing what a little change in the weather can do.

CHAPTER 11 : Surprising Collaborators

As the day was ending, I asked Brandon to stop by and talk with me before he left. When he showed up, he looked worried.

"What have I done now?" he asked. "Am I still in trouble about that Behavior Chart?"

"I think we're all figuring out how to solve that problem," I said.

Brandon scratched the side of his head. "Can I take that stupid thing down then?"

That question took me aback and I told him I'd have to talk it over with Carmen. "The reason I asked you to talk to me was just to say how much I liked how you handled that problem with Chad today. Where did you learn that?"

Brandon shrugged. "I guess from that friend of yours who came to our school, Dr. Goodwin, and the Choice Map and all that. Plus, I found out it really works at the skateboard park. It's like, well, see . . . I mean, you don't help little kids with their skateboarding if you keep threatening to send them to the principal's office."

I thought about this, then said: "Tell me something. How *do* you help little kids learn skateboarding?"

"I don't know. They have to really want to do it. They're just playing at first. You know, they see other kids doing it and it looks like fun, and they want to do it themselves. Then they start falling a lot. I make sure they're okay, and then I tell them to get back up and try again."

"Does that usually work?" I asked.

Brandon nodded. "Mostly. But sometimes they go Judger on themselves, you know, like on the Choice Map? Or some jerk makes fun of them. Then they get bummed. But I sort of coach them about Learner and you know what?"

"What?" I asked.

"If you know all that stuff about Judger and Learner, it's really easy to help them. That's what I'm finding out."

"How so?"

"I don't get bummed about their mistakes or other kids *dissing* them. I can do, like, 'oh, I'm going all Judger.' But I don't have to. I can ask them Learner questions like, what do you need to do right now to get better? That helps them go Learner. And it helps me, too. Right?"

"So this works with the kids and helps you in coaching," I said. "Is that it?"

"Pretty much, yeah. If you're going to ever get better at anything, you've gotta do that," he said, looking up as if remembering something. "It's a miracle that Becky ever got any good at skateboarding. I've never seen anybody be so Judger on herself. You know how she is, how she goes crawling into her shell." He laughed.

For a moment we were both quiet as I thought about what he was telling me. The truth is, I was bursting with excitement about what he was saying. This was one brilliant kid!

You know what, Mrs. Sheppard," he said, breaking the silence. "Remember that day on the playground when Becky got so mad at me for showing you those pictures of her skateboarding?"

"Sure, I remember. How could I forget *The Little Eagle?*"

"Yeah, really! Anyhow, after that, maybe a couple weeks, I guess I was sort of teasing her. I told her if she stopped being such a mean Judger on herself maybe she'd get good enough to go to the Olympics. Man, at first I thought she was going to go off on me for saying that but she laughed instead."

"She laughed?"

"I don't know if I should tell you this; it's sort of a secret. But not really. It's something she showed me, maybe it's an idea she got from the Choice Map. See, you get a little notebook, like this one, which is mine." He reached into his back pocket and pulled out a small spiral notebook wrinkled from much use. He flipped through a few pages to show me some notes he'd made.

"Becky showed me how to do it. At first, she'd always write down the things she didn't know how to do and all the times she messed up. She even made big black Xs for the bad days, when she did something really stupid and just wanted to quit. But then, after that day I showed you those pictures of her, she started doing something different. I guess maybe she actually realized she's really good, the way she can practically fly and all that. See, she started writing down days she calls her *high Learner* days or else her *high Judger* days. She says you've got to remember the things you connect with on those Learner days."

He quickly flipped through the pages of his own notebook, showing me some of the entries he'd made for himself. His scribbling made it difficult to see what he was working on and I didn't want to ask too many questions for fear that he'd get self-conscious and stop talking.

"See," he continued, "you start noticing you do best on the high Learner days. That's also when you have the most fun. It's very cool. It's actually pretty easy. You picture the Choice Map and where you want to go on it, Learner, Judger, whatever. You remember how it feels to be Learner, like she does when she flies like in those pictures. It really helps to have the map as a reminder. Look!" He flipped to the back cover of his notebook where he had made a rough sketch of the Choice Map.

"I guess you don't go to the skateboard park much, do you? But you should come sometime. Becky has gotten even better than those pictures you saw. And she smiles, too! That's a big deal. She smiles a lot."

He bowed his head and turned away to hide that he was blushing.

"Brandon," I said, "I think you've just helped me solve our problem with that Behavior Chart. You've given me a new direction to experiment with."

Brandon looked puzzled. "I have?"

"You sure have. It's about keeping those records about Judger days and Learner days and how we improve over time when we focus on Learner days.[20] I'll bet we can come up with something like that for our classroom. What do you think?"

"Well, it would sure be better than that stupid Behavior Chart," Brandon exclaimed. "A whole lot better! Are you really going to do it?"

"I think so," I said. "Yes. Definitely, yes."

"All right!" Brandon said. It was one of those long drawn out 'all rights' that was more sung than said. Then he grabbed his coat. "I gotta go," he said. He dashed out the door but a second later stepped back inside. "Mrs. Sheppard, it would be great if you took down the Behavior Chart."

"I still have to talk with Mrs. Santiago about it but I'm pretty sure she'll agree."

Brandon pumped his fists, gave a loud whispered *Yes*, then spun on his heel and disappeared down the hall.

I stood there for a long time, astonished by what had just happened. Finally I sat down at my desk and started jotting down notes as fast as I could. I could hardly wait to share all of this with Carmen, and with Sophie.

That evening after dinner, I tried calling Sophie again. There was a puzzling message on her answering machine. It was one of those pre-recorded voice messages announcing that Dr. Goodwin would be away until such-and-such a date. If urgent, messages could be left at 888-555-4321. Odd, I thought. Sophie hadn't mentioned that she was going away. But then I remembered all those boxes I'd seen last time I'd visited her apartment. I felt a little hurt that she hadn't told me she was going somewhere. Well, it wasn't like I was a family member or business associate. And while I would have loved to talk with her, my message certainly wasn't urgent. I made a mental note to call that number and find out when Sophie would be back, but not tonight.

I pressed my auto-dialer for Carmen and instantly got her voice mail message. When that happened my heart sank. I really wanted to share my excitement about Brandon with someone. I couldn't believe that neither Sophie nor Carmen were available.

What about Jared? I was sure he'd enjoy hearing about Brandon's breakthrough, even though I'd have to do a lot of explaining so he understood why it was such a big deal. Just then there was a light knock on my office door and Jared leaned inside. "Could I tempt you with an evening stroll?"

"This late at night?" I asked, noting it had gotten dark outside.

"Sure," he said. "There's a bright moon. Maybe it'll lift your spirits."

"I'm scared of the dark," I joked. "All kidding aside, some things happened in school today that I'd love to tell you about."

"Okay, then I'd love to hear about them," he said. He laughed, stepped into the room, and grasping both my hands, pulled me up from my chair.

CHAPTER 12

OPENING TO NEW POSSIBILITIES

*I never teach my pupils. I only attempt to provide
the conditions in which they can learn.*

Albert Einstein

Greenfield's Open House was a smashing success, with wonderful exhibits throughout the school. In our classroom, parents, teachers and kids crowded around our displays the whole evening, asking questions and talking with our students. From time to time our kids would come up to Carmen and me, telling us about exchanges they'd had with visitors. Similarly, parents stopped by to introduce themselves and say how wonderful it was to see their children so genuinely excited about school and proudly telling others about their projects. Any qualms I still had about being a teacher were behind me—well, mostly!

Marge Benson, a fifth grade teacher I knew only slightly, stopped to ask me about Brandon. "Last year, in my class, that boy was awful, a real handful," she said. "You can count your lucky stars that he's grown out of it." She tipped her head toward the front of the room where Brandon was chatting with two adults, pointing at the Choice Map that he and Becky had drawn on the white board that afternoon. I watched as he traced a line with his finger along the Judger path, then up the Switching Lane back to Learner. The adults standing beside him were totally engrossed.

"Yes, he is doing well," I told Mrs. Benson. I was eager to tell her about Carmen and our experiences with Brandon and what we'd done to help him change. Before I could get into it, she interrupted.

"Self-control," she said. "Somebody has finally gotten through to that child."

Just then she caught sight of her friend Biddy Privet and waved to get her attention. My heart sank as she excused herself and scurried off. I had wanted to suggest that she ask Brandon to tell her about the Choice Map. Earlier in the day he and Becky had worked together drawing the map on the board. Becky drew the map while Brandon drew two little figures in a box off to the side. The box was labeled "Judger Paths." One figure was of a turtle, the other a mean-looking bulldog. A bubble over the turtle's head said, "I go Judger on myself and crawl into my shell." A bubble over the bulldog's head said, "I go Judger by barking at other people."

Becky's drawing of the Choice Map had most of the same information as Sophie's, complete with figures on the paths and thought bubbles over their heads. Brandon had had her draw a caricature of himself climbing out of the Judger pit. "That's so kids will know there's a way to get out if they really mess up," he told her. "They don't have to stay down there forever." Becky's drawing of him was an amusing caricature. He had high-fived her when she was done.

After Becky completed the Choice Map, she drew a swooping arrow to the Learner Path with a banner that said, *Learner rocks!* Then she'd asked if I'd add a list of questions for switching from Judger to Learner. I knew the Switching questions I asked myself but it took a while to rephrase them for the kids. Here are the ones I gave Becky to write on her white board display of the Choice Map:

- Am I in Learner or Judger mindset right now?

- Am I listening with Learner ears or Judger ears?

- What will happen if I stay in Judger?

- What do I really want to happen? What would be best?

- How can I get out of the Judger pit?

Kim, who had put together a digital photo display, took pictures of Becky's Choice Map. She told me she was sending it out to everyone on her phone list. "Kids from other classes and everyone," she exclaimed, "can download it to their computers or phones or whatever. Maybe it'll go viral and be all over school." I must admit that I got swept up with her enthusiasm but later had second thoughts. What would the other teachers think about this—or about *me*?

Just before the doors opened for the parents and outside visitors, Dr. Marshall brought in a stack of 100 pocket-sized cards of the Choice Map that Sophie had given him for the Open House. By the end of the evening, all the cards were gone.

We had elaborate bulletin board displays with photos of activities the children were involved in outside of school. Most of them showed practical applications of things they were learning in school. The displays included everything from sports activities like Becky's skateboarding, to soccer, swimming, woodworking, computers, and even baking bread. There was a photo of a tree house one of the boys built with his father, a building contractor, complete with construction plans and calculations where we could clearly see how important it was to know math. There were science displays and Zak's CADD demonstration. One of the mothers, a graphic designer, had helped the children make a book of stories and poems that they had written themselves. It had been a perfect writing project, involving the whole class.

Many teachers visiting our room asked interesting questions. Most were enthusiastic about seeing the students' accomplishments and expressed surprise by their level of participation in the Open House. But not everyone was supportive. Three teachers walked briskly through the room, barely looking at either the displays or me. Biddy Privet was one of those. She pursed her lips and squinched up her face like she smelled something bad in our classroom. As we exchanged glances my shoulders got tense, and no doubt my lips started pursing up like hers. She paused long enough to tell me, in a most condescending tone, "Let me offer you a word of advice, young lady. Greenfield's Open Houses are intended to display our school's fine academic achievements. They're not an opportunity for children to show off how they amuse themselves outside school. You should be grateful Dr. Malstrom won't be seeing this. Now, there was a principal who knew how to run a school."

My jaw dropped. I was speechless. Biddy quickly turned on her heel and marched off. In that instant I went Judger on myself, feeling old self-doubts wash over me. Maybe I'd really messed up, like Biddy said. I glanced at that turtle Becky had drawn on the board, then took a deep breath to recover myself and ease back into Learner mindset.

During most of the evening, Dr. Marshall walked in and out of our room, greeting visitors and wearing a proud smile. He visited each display several times, chatting with our students and nodding his head with obvious interest. Twice he stopped by my side to talk about what he saw happening in our classroom.

"These are the kinds of changes I'm hoping to bring to the whole school," Dr. Marshall said. "Creativity, project-based learning, critical thinking and problem solving, everyone working together collaboratively, connecting with the 'whole child' and building on their strengths and interests, pride of accomplishment... you should be very proud of yourselves. You and Carmen have made some major changes here."

I nodded. "Sophie's way," I said. "You know that method she mapped out. It brings everything you just mentioned into focus for our kids—and for Carmen and me, too," I added, turning to my friend and smiling.

It was a great evening except for one thing: Sophie never showed up. I couldn't understand why, because I'd sent her three email reminders about it. She'd sent back an ambiguous reply about how she was certain it would be a wonderful event.

As the last visitors left our room, Dr. Marshall came in and closed the door behind him, making sure it was latched. He walked over to the table where Carmen and I were sitting, finally catching our breath, and pulled up a chair.

"There's something I need to tell you," he said solemnly. "It's not good news."

"Oh, no," I said. "It's about Sophie, isn't it?"

"I visited her two days ago," he said. "She didn't want me to tell you this until after the Open House. Perhaps you were aware that Sophie has had a serious health problem for a few years. Well, last week there was an emergency and now she's in hospice care at her daughter's home." He added quickly, "She's looking forward to a visit from both of you, the sooner the better."

Carmen and I just stared at him. I was stunned, the wind knocked out of me. After a few seconds, Carmen took my hand, held it to her cheek and said something in Spanish. Though I didn't understand the words, the tone of her voice was comforting.

The three of us sat in silence for a long time. Then we traded a few fond memories about Sophie and the impact she had had on each one of us. Carmen and I told Dr. Marshall how, when Sophie visited our class that day, she took command of the entire room the moment I introduced her. Her inviting presence won the children over immediately. She was kind, focused, curious, and interesting, bringing a collaborative spirit to us all. She had conveyed a powerful sense of respect for each child and it was obvious that they returned it in kind.

Jared arrived while we were still sharing stories about Sophie. When he saw the three of us sitting solemnly in the back of the room, he didn't say a word but leaned down to give me a hug.

We told him about Sophie and he shook his head in disbelief. "I'm so sorry," he said.

After a while I got myself together enough to take him through our Open House exhibits. The last thing I remembered that evening was Dr. Marshall taking pictures of the room. He was making up an album for Sophie, whom he was sure would be delighted with these mementoes. I had never lived through a day filled with such a mixture of joy, achievement, and sorrow.

Sophie's daughter met Carmen and me at the door and led us to the room which had been given over to Sophie's care. It was a bright, cheerful room with a large window overlooking the backyard. Sophie greeted us from a comfy recliner where she sat with a heavy blanket covering her legs. She looked grey and drawn but welcomed us cheerfully and was just as sharp and present as ever.

Sophie was filled with questions about the Open House pictures that Dr. Marshall had dropped off for her. She loved the photos of the Choice Map that Becky and Brandon had drawn and remarked how well they'd integrated the ideas into their own world. She smiled when I pointed out the words *Learner rocks!* that Becky had written at the top. Then she leaned in to examine the photo I handed her of Brandon in front of the drawing explaining the Choice Map to a group of adults.

"He's my little boyfriend," Sophie quipped. "I would have loved being his teacher but I know he's in good hands with the two of you. I hope you appreciate how much difference you're making in that child's life, though I'm sure he keeps you on your toes. The connection you have made with him, combined with what he's learning, is literally changing his life. You are changing his whole future."

"I hope so," Carmen said. "I'm still learning lessons about Learner mindset myself. You'd be surprised at how many times I go Judger on myself for the silliest things . . ."

Sophie laughed. "Yes. I couldn't have said it better myself."

I had so many things I wanted to talk about with Sophie. I wanted to share our successes with her. And there were still so many questions I had for her.

"You've got the basics now. The rest is up to you," Sophie said. "But it's easy to remember if you just think of a question mark and my favorite quote: *'The important thing is to not stop questioning.'*"

Carmen and I exchanged knowing glances, nodding in unison. What Sophie said had certainly proved to be true for us. As we developed our ability to create Learner weather, our students had become so much more engaged. They took more time with their lessons, were more careful and thoughtful. They became more openly curious and asked questions more freely when they had new ideas or wanted further clarification in lessons we were presenting.

Learning more about my students—their interests, the things they most loved to do outside school, and sometimes even the problems they were facing—took on a greater meaning for me. By seeing the bigger picture of their lives, I began asking different kinds of questions. While in Judger I'd primarily focused on what was wrong or missing; after shifting to Learner it really changed how I felt about them. It excited me to imagine their individual lives, and I got way more curious about them. I thought more about how to communicate with them in more meaningful and engaging ways. Now, nearly every day was filled with surprises—for all of us, I think.

"Who each child is, the whole child, has become increasingly important to me," I said. "I once heard someone say, 'it's not so much about *fixing* as it is about *relating*.'" I glanced at Carmen as I said this. With more than a little embarrassment, I realized how much I'd misjudged her in the beginning. By learning to shift out of my Judger mindset I had discovered a person who was not only a gifted teacher but who was now a good friend and treasured colleague.

"Carmen and I have become wonderful collaborators," I told Sophie. "It never could have happened without what you've taught us."

Sophie smiled, obviously pleased and touched. She spoke softly and it became increasingly difficult for her to express herself as our visit continued. Finally she said, "I want you both to promise me . . . to do everything you can to continue this work you've begun."

I took Sophie's hand. "This is the easiest promise I've ever been asked to keep," I said. Then I added, "Well, next to my promise to Jared, that is."

Sophie laughed quietly, raised her hand and made a circling gesture with her finger. "Just one other thing . . ."

"Always remember the question mark," I said, finishing the sentence for her.

"Yes," Sophie said. "Never stop questioning."

I couldn't have imagined how soon that promise I'd made to Sophie would be tested, and in the most personally challenging way possible. The first thing the next morning Dr. Marshall called on the classroom phone to tell me he was announcing a special staff meeting to discuss the Open House. He said there had been both praise and criticism concerning our displays. He wanted to make certain we were ready to respond to some very tough questioning by other members of the staff.

CHAPTER 13

STAFF MEETING SHOWDOWN

It's not differences that divide us.
It's our judgments about each other that do.
Margaret J. Wheatley

A few days after our visit with Sophie, Carmen and I walked into the multi-purpose room for the special meeting about our Open House. I loved the way the chairs had been deliberately placed in a large circle, so that we could each make eye contact with everyone else.

Dr. Marshall opened the meeting by congratulating us all on the success of our annual Open House. We'd had the best attendance in seven years, and he'd received a large number of laudatory phone calls and emails from parents. This was great news, and considering the comments I'd heard in our own classroom, I thought with satisfaction that Carmen and I had contributed to this feedback. But as I looked around the circle I could tell that not everyone agreed with Dr. Marshall. As he finished his short speech and asked for people's observations or questions, Biddy Privet's hand shot up.

"Yes, Ms. Privet," Dr. Marshall said, nodding in her direction.

Biddy launched into a rambling string of complaints about cell phones and messages being sent around that were very disruptive. "And," she proclaimed, "with all due respect, some of us don't agree with Dr. Marshall's appraisal of the Open House. Our goal at Greenfield has always been to showcase our best students' scholastic achievements. We have to assure our community that we're maintaining high academic standards. It was terribly ill-advised to ignore these objectives and parade out some of the students' outside activities instead."

I was shaken, I must admit. I looked around for the *we* that Biddy claimed to represent. Most people in the circle had put on a neutral face or were staring at the floor. I looked at Carmen who tipped back her head and rolled her eyes.

Biddy went on about academic standards and making young people accountable for their behavior. At one point her face turned so red I feared she'd have a stroke. Dr. Marshall listened respectfully. He seemed relaxed and unfazed by her comments. Biddy finally ended her speech, sat down and folded her hands in her lap, wearing a victorious expression. Dr. Marshall calmly asked if anyone else had questions or comments.

The next person to speak was Celia Jacobs, a teacher who'd been at Greenfield for many years.

"I do have some questions," she said, glancing in my direction. "I visited Mrs. Shepherd and Mrs. Santiago's classroom during our Open House and I was intrigued. Their children were all so engaged and excited about being there. And their exhibits were quite impressive, though they didn't always seem to follow the curriculum. I must say I loved seeing the kids so involved, though. It's like pulling teeth getting my students to participate in the Open House and to show up with their parents. What makes Emma and Carmen's students so different?" She stopped and got a funny grin on her face. "I know I'm a pretty good teacher so I've got to ask, what have they got that I don't?"

A restrained ripple of laughter went around the circle. Judging by Biddy's stony expression she did not appreciate Celia's humor.

"Maybe Emma and Carmen would like to answer that," Dr. Marshall said.

Every eye in the room turned in our direction. I glanced uncomfortably at the clock on the wall. We had only a few minutes to speak and I knew Carmen and I didn't have enough time to address the questions Biddy and Celia had raised. Then I had a sudden brainstorm. I dug into my bag and pulled out Sophie's manuscript. I'd flagged passages I wanted to share with Carmen. I quickly found what I was looking for and said, "I'd like to share something with you from a friend's writing." Then I proceeded to read from Sophie's journal:

Teaching is not just about subject matter but about communication, connection with our students and our ability to inspire their intrinsic motivation. That's what strengthens their becoming eager learners and achievers, even beyond what they might have thought possible. I can't emphasize enough the impact of the teacher's mindset on the climate of learning and achieving in the classroom, and on each individual child. We want so much for our students that I think we sometimes overlook the importance of each teacher managing his or her own mindsets in the face of all we have to deal with. Only then can we do the best job with our students and take care of ourselves, too. I often think of those pre-flight instructions we get on airplanes, to put on our own oxygen masks before trying to help anybody else.

I first created the Choice Map as a teaching aid for me, the teacher. I needed it to remind myself that I always have a choice about which mindset to teach from, even when things are hectic around me. Only later did I discover that the Choice Map, and the Learner and Judger mindset distinctions, could be helpful for my students too. I was thrilled with how intuitively they grasped the ideas and how this tool helped them become more open, thoughtful, curious, responsible, and studious.

I've always felt that teaching changes lives. Each of my students is indeed precious, every single one of them, no matter how they might appear. Each one of them deserves the best I have to give. How else might I expect to call forth the best in them?

While I, of course, care a great deal about academics, grades, and scores, what I care about the most is who my students are and the skills they must develop for living successful lives. What mindset will they need to become critical thinkers, problem-solvers, and true collaborators? As their teacher I have to be authentic and model these skills and not just talk about them. That's not easy for anybody. The Choice Map helps me stay on track.

Of course I recognize that nothing and no one is perfect. Given the very real challenges we teachers face these days, it is all too easy for us to go Judger on ourselves and our students. That's why I keep reminding myself that it's not about how often we go Judger; it's much more about how quickly we can recover ourselves and switch to Learner. Everything depends upon it.

I stopped reading, aware that the room had fallen silent. I looked up timidly, not sure what this meant. I relaxed a little when I saw that several people were nodding appreciatively.

Dr. Marshall thanked me, then said, "I wonder if you could give us some practical examples about how this works."

Carmen stepped in at this point. "Here's what I've seen since we began using the Choice Map," she began. "There have been many changes in our students, but two children in particular have made real breakthroughs. One was a child who rarely participated in class, who thoughtlessly dashed off her assignments and acted as though she didn't care about anything or anyone, including herself. She was a definite underachiever, barely earning Cs and doing her best to slip by unnoticed. Emma and I both noticed little clues that told us she could be doing much better. Frankly, we were both being a little judgmental about her. But she started to change only after our attitude about her changed first. It would take too long to go into all the details except to say that she's turned out to be quite gifted and is now actively participating in class, and turning in exceptional work."

"I know exactly who you're talking about," Biddy Privet interrupted curtly. "She's the one who doodled that map thing on your white board and now it's being circulated on cell phones. Someone even sent one to *my* phone. I do not find this constructive at all."

"Wait, I can speak to that," I said, turning to face her. "What you're calling a doodle is Becky's version of the Choice Map, a learning tool that was developed by the author whose work I was just reading to you . . ."

Dr. Marshall held up his hand. "I apologize for interrupting, Emma," he said. "But I promised to end this meeting on the hour and we're about to go over. However, before everyone leaves I have an announcement. As some of you know, we were planning on having a guest speaker for the professional development staff meeting I've mentioned to you. However, since the person I invited had to cancel, I'll be sending out notices when our new plans are firmed up."

I was startled that Dr. Marshall had cut me off like that,

since he was usually so respectful. I'd always felt that he valued my input but this was such an abrupt way to end the meeting. A group of other teachers closed in around him as I walked in his direction. John Jackson, the chair of our teachers' group, was telling him, "I hope you haven't forgotten our agreement about limiting unpaid, after school meetings."

"Not at all," Dr. Marshall answered.

They discussed the fact that the teachers had agreed to a limit of 12 hours of unpaid meetings for the year. What Dr. Marshall planned would take a few of those hours. "This is important material. I'm sure you'll all thank me in the long run."

With that settled, John and the others drifted away and Dr. Marshall turned to me. Carmen was now standing at my side.

"I'd like to speak with the two of you," he said, beckoning us to follow him to his office. He thanked us for how well we had handled ourselves in the teachers' meeting. Then he added, "You probably didn't know this but I had invited Sophie to present her Learner mindset system to our school. Sadly, she won't be able to do that now. However, she called this morning with an alternative plan. She suggested five people who can fill in for her."

"That's great," I said haltingly. "But who . . ."

Dr. Marshall got a big smile on his face. "Three of those people are right here in this room."

I reflexively glanced over my shoulder, fully expecting him to introduce us to three strangers. But all I saw was the open door.

"No entiendo!" Carmen exclaimed. "I don't understand. Are you talking about us? You, Emma and me? But you said five. Who are the other two?"

"Their names are Becky and Brandon," Dr. Marshall replied.

"Oh, dear," I said. "What a great idea!"

"Absolutely," Dr. Marshall said. "Who could be more qualified than the five of us? I've been incorporating Sophie's ideas into my own work for years and had already decided it was time to bring it to our whole staff. Emma, you can describe Sophie's work from two perspectives, as a student, and now, as a teacher applying her work with your own students. Carmen, you'll be perfect as the teacher newest to Sophie's process."

"And Becky and Brandon are the proof of the pudding," Carmen added.

"Indeed they are," Dr. Marshall said. "This will be a perfect mix."

"So that's why you cut me off in there," I said, still a bit perplexed.

"Yes, I do apologize for that," Dr. Marshall said. "Let's keep the material as fresh as possible until we're ready to present it. The other thing is, I really do need to honor my promise to close these after school meetings on time. Besides, that discussion with Ms. Privet could easily have become, shall we say, *open-ended*. So what about it? Can I count you in?"

I nodded and glanced in Carmen's direction.

"Sure, let's do it," she said. "But I'm a little nervous, I've got to say."

"No doubt we'll get some resistance but that's just part of working with change," Dr. Marshall said. "Oh, and will the two of you ask the kids and see how they feel about doing the presentation with us? That girl Becky is quite a little artist and Brandon did such a great job of explaining the basics of the Choice Map at the Open House. It would be great to have them aboard."

"Do you think they'll do it?" Carmen asked me.

"Stranger things have happened," I said. Truth be told,

I was concerned: would Becky and Brandon even consider it? Speaking to a group of teachers wouldn't be easy. Both kids had made great progress but were they ready for *this*? Who was I kidding? Was I ready for it myself?

CHAPTER 14

THE QUESTION THAT CHANGES EVERYTHING

And the day came when the risk to remain tight in a bud
was more painful than the risk it took to blossom.

Anais Nin

Prior to the professional development meeting that Dr. Marshall called, Brandon and Becky drew most of the Choice Map on the big white board in the multi-purpose room. Then they waited in the background as Dr. Marshall opened the meeting by handing out agendas with a copy of the Choice Map clipped to them. At his signal, Brandon and Becky wheeled the big white board into position for everyone to see. We watched in hushed silence as Becky sketched in some final details of the Choice Map.

As planned, Brandon was the chief spokesperson. He described, in his own words, some of the points illustrated on the map: "This guy is standing at the starting place," he said, pointing to the figure standing on the left near the junction of the two paths. "It's like something hits you and you can't decide where you're going to go with it." He walked his fingers along the Learner path for a short way to demonstrate. Then he glanced at me and made a swooping gesture with his arm along the Judger path. "This is the path where you can get into trouble."

I happened to glance over at Biddy Privet, who sat directly opposite me in the circle of staff members. Her eyes bugged out in disbelief as she watched what was unfolding before her. Brandon pointed to the figure climbing out of the Judger pit at the bottom of on the map.

"That's the pits," he said. "I used to get stuck down there a lot. Well, I still do sometimes."

Becky, who stood at the other end of the white board, nodded, pointing at Brandon with mock reproach as he talked about the Judger pit. I knew they had rehearsed this beforehand. Like real pros, Brandon even gestured back to Becky, as if to say, "Who, me?" That little pantomime of theirs even got a laugh and helped to lighten things up. Watching this, I couldn't help but think what a miracle it was that they had both come so far.

Brandon was amazingly poised. He actually seemed to be enjoying himself! "It's a bummer to get stuck in that Judger pit," he said. "Sometimes, stuff just happens, you know, and you go Judger. I used to get mad all the time. And I yelled a lot. Not that you mean to or anything. You just do. My teachers showed us how to get out of the pit, and that we can change. I never knew that before. And it's not as hard as you think." He made a wide gesture with his arms in front of the drawing and I was afraid he was going to ham it up.

Then Becky piped up, speaking clearly and confidently. I could hardly believe my ears. No longer withdrawn into her shell like a turtle, it was her soaring *Little Eagle* self who had shown up. "This whole thing," she said, "shows you how to stop yourself from landing in the Judger pit. It's about getting with the Learner path and what Mrs. Shepherd calls a Learner mindset."

Brandon fist-pumped and gave a little cheer: "All right!"

With that, the two children approached each other at the

center of the white board, high-fived, politely bowed and left the front of the room. There was a tentative patter of applause which slowly built as the children opened the door to leave. The clapping didn't drown out the victory whoops from Becky and Brandon as the door closed behind them. Then we heard their clambering feet racing down the empty hallway to the outside doors. I halfway expected to hear the shrill whistle of warning from the hall monitor but all was quiet.

All eyes in the room turned to Dr. Marshall standing by the white board, looking very pleased. He thanked Carmen and me for helping Brandon and Becky prepare, then handed the presentation over to us. We finished by going over the mindset material in the handouts. Dr. Marshall then spoke of scientific findings that demonstrated how different mindsets can affect the brain's ability to take in and integrate new information.

"The mindset we each bring to the classroom is an integral part of the educational process," he continued, "and this is something we may be tragically neglecting in this age of standardized tests and test-based learning. We need practical skills for creating a climate for learning, and that's what this mindset material can do. Each child knows when we're listening to them with Learner ears or Judger ears. Our own Learner mindsets orchestrate the quality of connection we have in our classrooms, which is rewarded by the greater attention, responsiveness, participation and mindfulness of each individual student.[21] As we work together with the Choice Map, I think you'll discover what a powerful tool it is for being the kind of teacher who makes a real difference in students' lives." He paused, gathering his thoughts. "All of us," he said, looking around the room, "can tell when we're being listened to with Learner ears or Judger ears. Look at what we're all dealing with these days— all the challenges of curriculum, standardized testing, different pedagogies, to say nothing of increasingly scarce resources. We need each other more than ever! Becoming better Learners isn't just for our students' benefit, it's also for each of us—and for all of us together. I believe this mindset material can be a major contribution toward creating professional learning communities that make all of our jobs easier and more rewarding."

The room fell silent as we took in Dr. Marshall's words. A gentle wave of applause passed around the room. The applause wasn't cautious so much as it was our way of marking a sincere and heartfelt moment. But Dr. Marshall wasn't done yet.

"Yesterday, while reviewing my notes, I came across a quote from an author I'm sure some of you are familiar with: Parker Palmer. He spoke of the most common questions we ask in education. The first is the *what* question: '*what* subjects shall we teach?' We go a little deeper and ask the *how* question: 'what methods and techniques are required to teach well?' Maybe we go deeper still and ask the *why* question: 'for what purpose and to what ends do we teach?' Then Dr. Palmer says, 'But seldom, if ever, do we ask the *who* question—who is the self that teaches? How does the quality of my selfhood form—or deform—the way I relate to my students, my subject, my colleagues, my world? How can educational institutions sustain and deepen the selfhood from which good teaching comes?'[22]

> Who is the self that teaches? How does the quality of my selfhood form —or deform—the way I relate to my students, my subject, my colleagues, my world? How can educational institutions sustain and deepen the selfhood from which good teaching comes?
> *Parker J. Palmer*

"How indeed *do* we sustain and deepen the selfhood from which good teaching comes," Dr. Marshall reflected. He looked down at his notes for a second and I had the distinct impression he was going to use that question to invite us into a discussion. But before he could say anything more, Biddy Privet was again waving her hand, this time with considerable agitation. She didn't even wait for Dr. Marshall to call on her.

Biddy leapt to her feet and pointed reproachfully at the white board: "As I said before, pictures of that map are circulating all over this school and I'm tired of it. It has nothing to do with education."

I was burning with something halfway between outrage and embarrassment by Biddy's remarks. Not only had she interrupted Dr. Marshall, obviously not hearing a word he'd just said, but you would have thought somebody was hatching a plot against Biddy herself. What harm could there be in sending pictures of the map to cell phones? How had they even gotten her number? Besides, her thinly disguised attack on Carmen and me, in front of our colleagues, was excruciating.

"Why would anyone think a drawing like this would fix anything?" Biddy exclaimed, getting increasingly wound up. "My goodness, we used to have such pride at this school. We had the highest academic scores in the district, but that's a thing of the distant past. What has happened to us? Nowadays, children think it's so smart to send secret texts and pictures to each other. We can't allow this while students plod along with Cs and Ds, and drop out by middle school. Why are we wasting our time with these *choosing maps* or whatever this business is all about?"

My head was spinning. Why was Biddy going after me and Carmen like this? Was she just picking on me because I was a beginning teacher and she thought I didn't know what I was doing? Never mind her attacks on me, I couldn't sit back and let her demean Sophie's work. I was determined to put that woman straight, but when I started to raise my hand, I felt accosted by self-doubts. How many other people thought as Biddy did?

That's when she got her second wind, this time going after Dr. Marshall. He seemed unperturbed, while I was getting more upset by the second.

"You're asking us to sit here for an unpaid, after-school meeting to discuss things that have nothing to do with why this school is in trouble," Biddy said, shaking her finger at Dr. Marshall. "Let's at least focus on the ABCs of good teaching. Apparently some people have forgotten the fundamentals."

Biddy's mention of the ABCs flipped a switch in my brain, reminding me of Sophie's ABCD Choice Process: *Aware. Breathe. Curiosity. Decide.* Okay, Emma, start with awareness. Am I in Judger? Are you kidding! Who wouldn't be, given Biddy's outrageous attacks? Now, *Breathe!* In my mind I stepped back to gain perspective. No. I certainly wasn't being objective. Not only that, I felt humiliated and angry and misunderstood. I exhaled slowly. Okay. What's next? Oh, right: *Curiosity.* What's really upsetting Biddy so much? And why is *her* behavior pushing *my* buttons? Just because Biddy was in Judger, did I need to go down to the pit with her? How can I turn this around? Biddy does have some valid points. What are my choices? Just then another question popped into my head: *Who do I choose to be in this moment?* Of course I have a choice. That was the whole point of what I'd been learning from Sophie. My next move suddenly became clear.

Who do I choose to be in this moment?

I raised my hand and heard Dr. Marshall call my name. Though I was trembling inside, I rose to my feet and the voice that came out was confident and steady. I began sharing the story you already know from reading this book, of how I'd seriously thought of quitting being a teacher, even though it had been my dream for such a long time. I told how I'd been overwhelmed by the problems we are facing in education, and the challenges of reaching difficult kids. I said I'd felt so burdened that I wasn't able to connect with my students as I wanted, or give them what they needed most, to learn how to think and reason for themselves. I told how I'd started to believe that being a good teacher today was simply impossible—at least for me.

As I spoke, I was aware of heads nodding in concurrence around our circle. I sighed with relief. Others had experienced what I'd been going through. That affirmation touched me, encouraging me to continue. I told them about meeting Sophie again, so many years after she had been my sixth grade teacher, and of how her early lessons with the Choice Map had changed my life. I felt myself tearing up. But I took a deep breath and managed to go on. I told them how Sophie had helped me more recently with the dilemmas I was facing as a teacher. This not only helped me personally but gave me a choice about who I am when I walk into that classroom each morning. Sophie had been the teacher who changed my life, and it was my dream that my students could say that about me someday. That's when I really did choke up. The whole room became silent.

After a few seconds I added how Carmen and I had used Sophie's material to build a true collaboration that had a positive impact not only on our kids' academics but on their behavior and how they treated each other. I shared what I'd learned about recognizing my own mindsets and how the Choice Map provided a *practical mental tool* that helped me choose my mindset to connect better with my students as well as with fellow staff members. All of this reinforced what Dr. Marshall had said about teachers creating the *weather* not only in the classroom but throughout the school. Before I'd finished everything I wanted to say, Celia Jacobs raised her hand and I called on her.

CHAPTER 14 : The Question that Changes Everything

"I'm right with you," Celia said. "There's probably no one here who hasn't gone through their own version of the doubts you've described. And who *doesn't* want to be the kind of teacher who changes lives?" Quiet murmurs of agreement rippled through the room. Then Celia said, "I also want to say this. It's already obvious that you and Carmen are changing lives. I saw it in your students at our Open House. So, I know one thing for sure, I'd really like to know more about mindsets and give those ideas a try in my classroom."

I was elated. I quickly glanced around the room, not sure of the others' reactions and still a little worried about Biddy. People were leaning forward, waiting to hear more. I looked at Biddy. Was it my imagination that even she was listening with interest?

I don't remember the exact sequence of events that occurred once I started responding to Celia's question. I was relieved when Carmen entered the conversation, and we described how the children were changing as we changed and about the liveliness and excitement of our classroom. "Now I love coming to school in the morning," Carmen said. "Working with Emma is so satisfying. Mostly, I love working with the children, watching their minds come alive with learning and discovery, asking questions, and understanding so much more." She paused and looked down at her notes. "It's like what Dr. Marshall said about good teaching and deepening the selfhood from which it comes."

Then Dr. Marshall stepped in, telling us it was time to stop, since he had promised to end the meeting on the hour. Some people groaned in protest, wanting to continue. Others had time commitments and needed to leave, so we voted to adjourn.

"Is it fair to assume that all of you would like to continue these discussions?" Dr. Marshall asked, smiling broadly. There was unanimous agreement. Even Biddy nodded approval! One teacher asked, "Will there be more handouts or perhaps a workbook to help us out?"

"Definitely there will be more handouts," Dr. Marshall said. "As for a workbook, that may take more time." He looked at me and raised his eyebrows as if to say, *Good idea, don't you think?*

When Dr. Marshall dismissed the meeting and thanked us for our presentation, the group actually applauded. I felt my face flush, a little embarrassed, but I must say that I was really pleased. I hadn't expected that.

Carmen and I exchanged a few words, congratulating each other on our accomplishment and then she rushed off to pick up her niece, Darlina. I was nearly to my car when I realized I'd left behind the journal with all my notes. I ran back inside to the multipurpose room. It was already dark in there except for the dim security lights in the ceiling. The chairs hadn't been moved since our meeting so I had no trouble locating where I'd been sitting. I picked up my journal and stuck it in my tote bag. I was about to leave when I heard a slight rustle off in the shadows.

"Emma, please wait a moment." The voice was just barely a whisper. I stared into the darkness. I was astonished to realize it was Biddy Privet. "I didn't mean to frighten you," she said. She walked back into the circle and rearranged a chair so it faced the one I'd been sitting on earlier. "Please, can we talk?" she asked.

I tentatively sat down facing her, not knowing quite what to expect. She reached into the shallow pocket of her skirt for a tissue. "I'm so ashamed of being seen like this," she said. After a quick intake of breath she added: "You won't tell anyone, will you?" Then she quickly added: "Oh, heck, I don't care. I'm just not going to worry about keeping up appearances anymore.

"I just need to share something with you, Emma. First, I want to apologize for being so unpleasant to you this afternoon, and last week in that other meeting as well," she said. "I know I'm not the friendliest person. But when I visited your room during Open House, I have to say I found it quite challenging—actually disturbing, to tell the truth." She blew gently into her tissue. "You have such wonderful rapport with your students. And you've done wonders with Brandon, who everyone knows has been a problem since he first came to this school. He's always been so rude as we pass in the hallways. As for that girl Becky, she's such a quiet thing. Then when you and Carmen were talking this afternoon, and those two children acted so differently, a light went on in my brain. It's made me question so many things about my years of teaching, that my mind is in a jumble. Sometimes it terrifies me to look at myself. As you may know, I'll be retiring next year, and this has suddenly caused me to wonder about things I've never thought about before. I'm so sorry. I've never been one to bother others with my personal matters but I thought you might understand."

"Biddy, listen, if I've said anything to hurt you, I apologize . . ."

She reached out, touching my arm. "Oh, you're not to blame at all. Just the opposite." She quickly withdrew her hand, as if she'd done something wrong. For a moment the two of us sat in silence. Finally she said, "Maybe I'd better leave."

Biddy started to get up, but I reached out to touch her hand. "Please go on," I said.

"If you're sure it's all right," she said, settling back in her chair. "Here I am close to retirement, and I'm discovering new things that would have made all my years of teaching so much more satisfying. I've never thought much about mindsets, much less that changing them was possible." She stopped and took a deep breath.

"My students did very well in their academics," she continued. "I'm proud of that. But we all know that a child's education must include so much more than good grades in today's world. That must sound strange coming from me. Most people think I'm awfully set in my ways, and I admit that I am. But I'm also not blind to my own shortcomings. I want to learn more about what you and Carmen and Dr. Marshall were talking about today. Plus, you know, the changes in those two children simply astounded me. I wouldn't have believed it possible if I hadn't seen it with my own eyes. I've always believed—how does that old saying go, that you can't change a leopard's spots? But you know, in a way it's exciting, like being young again, and having a realization that changes your life. Still, I wish I'd known about these ways of thinking forty years ago. I'm sure my life would have turned out very differently."

I nodded. "I think I understand," I said. "But is it enough to know all this now?"

"Oh, yes, more than enough," Biddy said. "I would hate to have ever missed this."

We gathered up our things and left the building together. On the way out she asked, "Could we meet again and talk about what you learned from your Dr. Goodwin? I have so much to catch up on."

Her question took me aback. She, a senior teacher, was asking *me* about how to teach! "I'm hardly qualified, but I'm sure that Sophie..." Whatever I was going to say after that was choked off by a sob.

"What is it?" Biddy asked. "Are you all right, dear?"

"I'm fine," I said, taking a deep breath to recover. "I was going to say that Dr. Marshall has scheduled meetings for all of us to talk about this material. He's much more qualified than I, though I'll certainly contribute what I can."

"I look forward to that," Biddy said. "Oh, one more thing.

CHAPTER 14 : The Question that Changes Everything

What was that question Dr. Marshall said he asks himself?"

I thought and then said, "Who do I choose to be at this moment?"

"Yes," Biddy said, enthusiastically. "That does change everything, doesn't it?"

We were standing near the sidewalk that went up to the parking lot. I asked Biddy if I could give her a lift somewhere.

"No, thank you," she said. "I live only a few blocks away. I'll enjoy the walk. There's so much to reflect on."

Before turning to leave, she reached out and gave me a furtive hug. I was so surprised I forgot to say goodbye.

EPILOGUE

THE FIVE QUESTIONS

Each time I walk into a classroom,
I can choose the place within myself
from which my teaching will come,
just as I can choose the place within my students
toward which my teaching will be aimed.

Parker J. Palmer

The day after the teachers' meeting, I visited Sophie for the last time. Heather, her daughter, ushered me into the bedroom where her mother was sleeping, and touched Sophie's shoulder gently, telling her I was there. Sophie's eyes fluttered open and she smiled, inviting me to sit down in a chair beside her bed. She was surprisingly eager to hear about our presentation at the school meeting. Typical of her, Sophie's passion for education never faded, not even in those final days. I told her about Brandon and Becky drawing the Choice Map for the teachers. I even told her how I'd nearly been hijacked by Judger when Biddy Privet did her thing, and that unexpected private conversation we'd had after the staff meeting.

"Ah, Ms. Privet! Your nemesis, or former nemesis," Sophie said, with a little grin. "Funny how some people think it's an either-or proposition—curriculum *or* creating a climate for learning. You can't separate them, can you?" She waved her hand, as if flicking away a fly. "You know what I mean, don't you?"

"Yes," I said. "I do."

"I hope you've remembered my offer," she said, reaching out for my hand. "I've put everything together for our project. It's a bigger task than we thought. But you'll do fine. Heather will take you to the apartment. Everything is there."

I gave Heather a puzzled look.

"Mother said you're writing the workbook," Heather said. "I helped gather together the files you'll need."

"Oh, of course," I stammered. "But I'm just a beginner. How can I do it without . . . without you?"

"Shush," Sophie said, putting a finger to her lips. "You'll do just fine. It's been incubating in your mind . . . since you were in the sixth grade. Besides, Carmen and Dr. Marshall will be there to help you."

I laughed in spite of the seriousness of the moment. "As usual, you're right," I said, leaning across Sophie's bed to give her a gentle hug.

"Take my word for it," she said. "You'll do great."

Our eyes met and an intimate silence filled the room.

A few weeks after Sophie's passing, I returned to her apartment and started going through the boxes of monographs and notes she'd left for me. Heather said her mother had arranged for me to use the apartment for three or four months so I could have access to her books before they were turned over to the university library.

It was during this same period that Dr. Marshall scheduled meetings for the staff to learn more about Sophie's work. He led most of these after-school meetings and brought in sections of the workbook, getting everyone's feedback. Those meetings provided a perfect laboratory for testing and refining the 12 tools in the evolving workbook. Together we were generating ideas that none of us would have come up with on our own.

I often worked alone at Sophie's apartment, long into the night. Sometimes Jared came to keep me company, reading or doing his own work. Carmen came occasionally, too, and was great at helping me figure out exercises connected with each tool. Being there in the room where Sophie had lived and worked was exactly the right setting for me to finish our "collaboration."

Reading through Sophie's journals and notes, as well as my own, I selected some of the most meaningful questions Sophie had given me. Putting them together, I realized that this list of five questions could guide me not only in the classroom but everywhere in my life. That's why I made a small poster of those questions and put it in a picture frame. Now it's hanging on the wall in my home office, right next to the Choice Map.

The Five Questions

1. What do I want—for both myself and others?

2. Am I in Learner mindset or Judger mindset right now?

3. Am I *listening* with Learner ears or Judger ears?

4. What assumptions am I making?

5. Who do I choose to be in this moment?

It was not unusual, in the course of putting together the tools for Sophie's workbook, to remember bits and pieces of conversations I'd had with her. Whenever I needed to clarify something, I imagined her right there with me. I didn't feel shy about asking my questions out loud—and even taking Sophie's side to answer myself! Anyone eavesdropping might have thought I'd lost my marbles.

One day, I imagined telling Sophie that it would be great to have some kind of simple self-coaching format to follow for applying her system. I pictured a logical sequence of questions to ask myself to help me learn from my mistakes without spending a lot of time in Judger. I also thought it might help me counsel students to get back to Learner mindset after they'd made a mistake or gotten a poor grade.

"Well, Emma," I heard myself telling myself in my imitation of Sophie's voice: "I guess if you want a *do-it-yourself format*, you'll just have to—*do it yourself!*"

I laughed out loud, thinking how typical that answer would have been from my friend Sophie.

I dove in, and after a couple of hours, put together what I'd been imagining. I was delighted with the outcome. I now had a simple process that integrated the Choice Map and Sophie's other mindset tools. I showed it to Carmen. She tested it and loved it too.

The next time our teachers' learning group got together, we had an especially lively meeting talking about the process. They took copies of the instructions home and used them to learn from their own mistakes and failures, to search for new ideas, and to work out new ways of using a particular curriculum. They used the instructions for exploring more collaborative relationships with other teachers, parents, and even within their own families. Celia Jacobs shared how she'd used it with a student who'd failed a test. Even though at first he was very Judger and down on himself, when they looked at the Choice Map he made up a Switching question that turned things around for him. After asking himself, "Am I willing to ask for help?" he and Celia worked out a plan for him to catch up and he got a B+ on his next test.

I call the self-coaching format I developed that day, a *"Reflection Scenario for Learning from Mistakes."* You'll find it in the *Workbook of 12 Mindset Tools,* which follows. It's the very first tool there.

Eight years have passed since the day I began teaching at Greenfield. Carmen and I continued co-teaching sixth grade for two more years after Sophie died. Then we were assigned our own classrooms. Under Dr. Marshall's direction, Greenfield regained its academic rating as one of the top schools in the district. But more than that, it became a rich and enjoyable place of learning for students and staff alike. I love being here. It's exciting just to walk in the front door, greet the kids and other teachers, and know that we share something very special.

There are days when I still miss co-teaching with Carmen, but we get together often. Sometimes we bounce ideas around, including how we're going to handle certain curriculum and teaching challenges.

Dr. Marshall recently had an article published on professional collaboration and how our teachers' learning groups have made such a difference at Greenfield. "One thing we've learned for sure," he said in that article. "Teachers need each other, for our own sakes as well as for our students' learning and advancement."

Since eight years have passed at the time of this writing, you may be wondering what has become of Brandon and Becky.

Brandon went on to college and is a coaching assistant for the university's football team. Becky set her sights on becoming a graphic designer and recently started an internship with a leading educational publisher.

As for Biddy, she did retire, spent many months traveling, and then returned to Greenfield as an on-call volunteer for the school. She's still a very private person, but from time to time we get together for lunch, and swap stories about teaching. And, yes, she did change her way of being with students. As she likes to remind me, always with a twinkle in her eyes, "Don't ever let anyone tell you a leopard can't change its spots."

Dr. Marshall is thoroughly dedicated to our school and to making a difference in education in general. When he was first assigned to Greenfield, our school was *in transition,* actually on the list of schools to be closed. But that's no longer the case. Instead, our student population has expanded along with our reputation for academic excellence. Four portable classrooms have been added and a new building is being planned.

Because of his success with turning our school around, Dr. Marshall is much in demand as a speaker. I recently attended an educational conference where he was presenting the keynote speech. I guess he always begins the way he did that day, by sharing stories about Sophie Goodwin and her impact on him, personally and professionally. He showed slides of the Choice Map, explained her mindset system and handed out a sampling of the tools from our workbook. The day I attended the conference, he ended with the following, which I recorded:

"In my heart of hearts," he said, "I'll always be a teacher, whether I'm in the classroom, meeting with parents, or carrying out my administrative responsibilities. Wherever I am, I always try to keep those *who-am-I-being* questions at the top of my mind."

Those words brought back memories of so many experiences and conversations I'd had with Sophie. I thought of how profoundly her ideas and lessons have enriched my own life and what I'm now able to bring to my own students. It is difficult to remember those months of personal doubt about becoming the kind of teacher that Sophie had been for me. She truly changed my life, not only for the sixth grade, but also for my adulthood as a teacher and a human being.

I hope that in telling this story and offering the workbook that follows these pages, Sophie's wisdom and practical gifts will bear fruit for each and every reader and through you, spread to those people whom you touch in your life.

12 MINDSET TOOLS FOR IGNITING THE LOVE OF LEARNING

This workbook presents the 12 tools of the Learner Mindset System, within which the story of Emma Shepherd was framed. Because these tools are *life skills*, compatible with how our brains take in new information and learn, you'll discover they can make a positive difference in every moment and area of your life, both professionally and personally.

These tools have proven useful in a wide variety of organizational and educational settings. They are ideal for more productive conversations with professional learning communities as well as with students, other staff members, and in your personal life.

Over the years, my students and clients have shared hundreds of stories about breakthroughs they've made simply by posting Choice Maps on bulletin boards, as Emma did in the story, sharing them with colleagues and teams, or putting them on their refrigerators at home. The Choice Map is central to this mindset and questioning work, so it's a perfect way of introducing others to the benefits of these practices.

Each tool complements and reinforces the others, so you can work through them in the order presented, or just dive in wherever you like, using the Choice Map as the basic structure and focal point for the system. Because it illustrates the core principles of this system, the map quickly guides you to the Learner mindset should you get hijacked by Judger or just want to refresh your memory of these skills.

The first and last tools of the workbook are like "bookends": The first tool is *Reflection Scenario for Learning from Mistakes;* the last tool is *Collaborate with Professional Learning Communities (PLCs).* The *Reflection Scenario* is a journaling exercise for individual learning, while *Collaborate with Professional Learning Communities* is an overview of how these tools can be used in collective, collegial study and practice. Whether you are a member of a professional learning community, participate in a book club, or perhaps have a less formal learning relationship with a colleague, you'll find this workbook a valuable asset for benefiting from the same skills Emma, her colleagues and her students learned from Sophie Goodwin in *Teaching that Changes Lives.*

I'd love to hear from you. I'm especially interested in stories about ways this book and the tools of the Learner Mindset System have made a difference in your own life.

From time to time I'll be posting new resources and other materials related to *Teaching that Changes Lives* at my website: (www.InquiryInstitute.com). Please visit often.

THE TOOLS

REFLECTION SCENARIO FOR LEARNING FROM MISTAKES

Our mistakes are the growing pains of our wisdom.

Anonymous

How often have you heard some version of the above adage? As valuable as that advice may be, it's not always clear how to *apply* it so you can learn and grow from your own mistakes. The following journaling exercise, with its format of six questions, is an excellent place to start. Writing often clarifies our thinking, and keeping a journal provides a valuable record to remind ourselves of our insights and growth.

The first question of this tool asks you to think of a recent experience in which you believe you failed or made a mistake. With that experience in mind, follow through with the other five questions in the Scenario.

Ask and answer each question in the order presented, and in the first person. If other questions occur to you along the way, be sure to include them as they will be especially valuable.

As you become familiar with this tool, you'll discover other applications for it, for example, to guide an individual student out of the Judger pit and back to Learner mindset, or to guide conversations with colleagues, in a professional learning community, or with friends, or with family members.

It's best to do this exercise when you can focus on it without interruption.

1. What is the *situation* in which I believe I made a mistake or failed? Why was success in this situation important to me and/or to others? What were the consequences of not achieving the success I wanted?

2. What were my *original goals* in this situation—for me, for others and for the situation in general? If I'm not sure how to answer this, did lack of clarity about goals contribute to the problem—and in what ways?

3. What *assumptions* did I make about my goals, other people or the situation? How might those assumptions have contributed to this mistake or misunderstanding?

4. How might my *Judger questions* have impacted other people and the outcome of the situation? What were the *costs* of Judger?

5. With the *Choice Map* in mind, what questions *could* I have asked myself to get on the *Switching Lane* and *shift to Learner mindset*?

6. If I could replay that situation now, what would I do differently? *What have I learned* so I can achieve more satisfying outcomes now, and in the future?

TOOL 2

MINDFULNESS: EMPOWERING YOUR OBSERVER

Purpose: To reinforce your ability to be calm and present with yourself and others, moment by moment. *Mindfulness* promotes a greater sense of equanimity and "centeredness," making it possible to think about your thinking in real time. With practice, you'll become more flexible, resourceful, awake, and intentional—*responsive* rather than *reactive*. For centuries, philosophical, psychological, and spiritual traditions have actively employed mindfulness practices that promote the ability to detach in a healthy way from one's own thoughts and feelings, simply noticing *what is*. As Sophie told Emma, with practice you'll begin to "see things in a neutral and open-minded way, like watching a movie of your life rather than being caught up in it."

Discussion: We can never become completely objective, neutral and open, but the observer mode helps us build our immunity to distracting Judger thoughts and feelings, and thus become able to solve problems more effectively, negotiate change more easily, and operate more calmly under pressure. These are invaluable skills for creating a Learner climate in the classroom, where there are infinite occasions for getting *hijacked* by Judger!

Practice #1: Sit in a comfortable, straight-backed chair, shoulders relaxed, hands resting comfortably in your lap. Inhale slowly and gently through your nose, picturing your lungs filling, almost as if they are doing it themselves. Let your abdomen expand. Mentally count slowly from one to four, feeling your whole body relaxing. Exhale comfortably and slowly through your nose, mentally counting slowly from one to four again. Be at ease, aware of your body softening, relaxing. Continue breathing in this way for three minutes or so. If your thoughts wander, simply shift your attention back to your breathing.[23]

Practice #2: Cultivate your *observer self* by continuously, calmly, and non-judgmentally asking yourself this single question: *What's present now?*

Practice #3: The next time your phone rings or you get a text, just allow yourself to be still instead of answering. Notice any thoughts that occur and how it feels to be still, without even peeking to find out who's contacting you. Simply observe what's going on in your mind and body. You might find it helpful to imagine that your thoughts and feelings are like clouds moving across the sky as you calmly observe them. Just *be*.

CULTIVATE CURIOSITY

Purpose: To rev up your Inquiring Mindset. Driven by our curiosity we begin learning about ourselves and the world around us long before we're introduced to any kind of formal learning. Einstein once said: "I have no special talent. I am only passionately curious." He is a model for cultivating the tenacious curiosity that fuels creativity, imagination, and discovery. Because curiosity is so easily stifled, it is essential to continuously cultivate it.

Discussion: Emma described how her life changed as Sophie's sixth grade student. She began to feel that her curiosity, her ideas and her questions were worthwhile, and so was she. Sophie later explained that Emma had reawakened her *curiosity-and-questioning mode* when she freed herself from the Judger thinking which had stifled her natural inquisitiveness.

Exercise #1: Watch an infant or young child. Notice those moments of fascination, wonder, and curiosity-driven exploration as young children learn about things you now take for granted, like reaching out and touching an object, starting to walk, or encountering new experiences or sensations for the first time.

Exercise #2: Get curious about *yourself.* Get curious about curiosity and the role it plays in your life. Throughout the day, notice which activities and people arouse your curiosity and which do not. Pay attention to the *experience* of curiosity as well as what, or maybe who, stifles it.

Exercise #3: Reimagine everyday objects. Creativity and innovation are fueled by deep curiosity and persistent questioning. Select some everyday object to focus on such as a paperclip, a bowl, or a cell phone. How many purposes can you imagine for that object besides the one(s) for which it was intended? If you were a different person, say a dentist, rap singer, or rocket scientist, what different things might you be curious about regarding this object? What different questions might you ask in the case of each object?

Exercise #4: Become an explorer and researcher. Imagine that you have just landed on planet Earth from a faraway solar system, and *everything* you encounter is unfamiliar. Somehow you know you're safe and thus able to freely exercise your curiosity. What would you be curious about? What questions would you ask about phenomenon such as gravity, color, movement, sound, or the purpose of different objects? What questions would you have about various people you encounter?

Exercise #5: Welcome wonder and awe into your life. With the openness of a child, take time to be with everyday wonders, perhaps the miracle of a sunset, the color and fragrance of an exquisite flower, or the experience of seeing a newborn for the first time. I often recall that moment of awe in the movie *The Miracle Worker,* when Helen Keller, born blind and deaf, first discovers language by associating the word *water* with the *experience* of water. Recall and revel in similar wondrous experiences in your own life.

GROW YOUR INQUIRING MINDSET

Purpose: To increase the quantity and quality of the questions you ask yourself and others, and to cultivate the field from which new questions arise. This tool is aimed at reinforcing the *habit* of asking questions, becoming more comfortable and patient with "not knowing," and underscoring the importance of reflection before action. This exercise helps you grow your inquiring mindset and your ability to be in the "questioning zone," deepening your habit and ease with asking questions of yourself and others.

Discussion: Think of an inquiring mindset as the habit, curiosity, and courage of asking open-minded questions of oneself and others. Each of these three descriptors contributes to a classroom climate most conducive to learning, thoughtfulness, collaboration, and accomplishment. An inquiring or questioning mindset aligns us with Learner, while a "certainty mindset" aligns us with Judger. Recall the climate of excitement, learning, and questioning in the classroom as Emma and Carmen's students prepared for their Open House.

Practice #1: Look around and select any random object your gaze falls upon. Now, *going for quantity not quality*, write down as many questions about that object as you can in one minute. Do this practice every day for a week, picking a different object each time. Make a game of it, seeking to increase the number of questions with each succeeding day. Keep a record and see how you do!

Practice #2: A variation of Practice #1 is to focus on a different *person* each day, generating more questions each time.

Practice #3: When someone asks you a question, perhaps looking for advice or a quick-fix solution, become curious and ask them questions instead of automatically answering. For example, ask clarifying questions about the situation, their goals, what they've already tried, or what they may want you to provide.

TOOL 5

QUESTION ASSUMPTIONS

Purpose: To create a constructive habit of discovering and challenging assumptions that could otherwise cause problems, blind spots, and limitations.

Discussion: Making assumptions is like wearing blinders without realizing they're even there. Assumptions and hidden beliefs are our largest sources of problems, misunderstandings, and missed opportunities. Making assumptions is just part of being human, so you can assume you're always making them just like everyone else. The best defense against problems and limitations caused by assumptions is to cultivate your inquiring mindset, stay curious, and continuously ask questions. Most important, the habit of questioning assumptions is a fundamental discipline for becoming an effective creative and critical thinker.

Remember Emma's assumption that something must be wrong with Becky for getting angry when Emma told her she had "potential." Similarly, Emma and Jared learned to correct faulty assumptions with each other, as well as with co-workers, leading to more effective communication and more satisfying relationships. Until we question our assumptions they can sabotage our efforts to achieve our goals and deepest desires. Begin with marshaling the courage and willingness to discover and investigate your own assumptions.

Exercise #1: Think of a problem you had with another person that still baffles you. Stay in Learner mindset as you wonder about any assumptions you and the other person might have been making. If this involved a student, you might ask what assumptions you made about his or her desire or ability to learn, or why this student might have not understood something you said.

Exercise #2: Assumptions and relationships. Think of a relationship you would like to improve with a student, colleague, friend, or family member. Ask assumption-busting questions such as the following:

- How would I describe what's going on right now with myself and the other person?

- What assumptions am I making about this person, including what they said or did?

- How can I check out my assumptions in an appropriate and kind way?

- What are the facts?

- Without those assumptions, what might I learn, understand, and appreciate about him or her?

- Am I willing to think of and relate differently with this individual?

- What new possibilities might open up for each of us?

Exercise #3: Changing your own possibilities. Think of a situation where you feel you've hit a wall or have tried everything to improve things but to no avail. Perhaps you feel hopeless about changing the situation or yourself. Step back, make sure you're in Learner mindset, and get very curious about what negative assumptions and beliefs may be blocking your progress. Experiment by creating some positive assumptions and discover how these open the door to new thinking and possibilities.

BUILD A RESILIENT LEARNER MINDSET

Purpose: To reliably bounce back when you get temporarily hijacked by Judger thoughts and feelings. Operating with a resilient Learner mindset means you won't be easily toppled by Judger thoughts or even a Judger highjack, or at least not for long. Your ability to bounce back will be strengthened by building your immunity to Judger negativity, whether those triggers come from yourself or someone else.

Discussion: A Judger hijack can only succeed when you believe that any critical Judger opinions about you—your own or someone else's—are actually true. Just as with strengthening any muscle, building a resilient Learner mindset requires ongoing practice. You can learn to simply "be with" Judger rather than behaving like the proverbial *puppet on a string*, controlled by your Judger thoughts, feelings and reactions. You may recall how Emma's resilient Learner mindset helped her stay in Learner and defuse the effect of Biddy Privet's attacks in the two teacher meetings.

Exercise #1: Imagine you're completely protected by an invisible bubble, immune to any Judger comments or opinions that come your way. Standing inside that bubble, you enjoy watching the "slings and arrows" that are hurled in your direction as they hit this protective barrier and bounce off, landing in feeble piles on the ground.

Exercise #2: Recall Sophie and Emma's conversations about not labeling ourselves or others, and how Learner and Judger are descriptions of *mindsets, not* people. As Sophie says: "We are all recovering Judgers." When Emma becomes frustrated with herself for "going Judger," she remembers Sophie's advice to "make friends with Judger." Accept Judger as just part of being human. The more accepting we are towards Judger—in ourselves and others—the more freedom we gain. This awareness and acceptance of Judger mindset is the transformational key for easily and quickly switching from Judger to Learner.

TOOL 7

LISTEN WITH LEARNER EARS

Purpose: To amplify your ability to listen with Learner ears, which is sometimes called *generous listening*. This fundamental skill helps establish a Learner climate: (a) in the classroom, to promote student engagement and accomplishment; (b) with colleagues and in professional learning communities, to promote collaborative relationships and more open creative sharing of knowledge and resources; and (c) in our personal lives, to promote more satisfying and successful relationships.

Discussion: It's easy to take listening for granted, to assume that listening is something that just happens automatically and that we hear what is objective and "really there." It's enlightening to realize that we *choose how we listen* and that this choice affects what we hear. In the story, Jared came up with the term "listening with Learner ears" when he was telling Emma about Mickey, the co-worker whose behavior irritated him so much. Jared developed a more constructive working relationship with his colleague when he was able to "take off my Judger ears and start listening with Learner ears." When Emma put on her Learner ears at school, she had major breakthroughs, perceiving Carmen, Brandon, and Becky in positive new ways. Sophie expressed a similar theme when she told Emma: "Learner begets Learner and Judger begets Judger."

Exercise #1: Listening with Learner ears is a matter of identifying the questions we're listening with and changing those questions if we want better outcomes. For example, imagine that you're listening to a speech—or to a student or colleague. Start by listening with the question: "What's wrong or stupid about what that person is saying?" What answers will you get? Then switch to listening with the question, "What's right and brilliant about what that person is saying?" What answers will you get this time? What was different about what you heard, depending on whether you were listening with Learner ears or Judger ears?

Exercise #2: Recall a time when it felt like someone was *listening to you with their Judger ears*. What was the situation? How did you feel about the other person and yourself? What do you imagine that person was assuming about you at the time? What were the outcomes of that experience?

Exercise #3: Recall a time when it felt like someone was *listening to you with their Learner ears*. What was that experience like? How did you feel about the person and yourself? What did you imagine the other person was assuming about you at the time? What were the outcomes of that experience? In what ways was this experience different from the Judger one in Exercise #2?

Exercise #4: Bring to mind a recent situation when you found yourself in Judger mindset, listening with Judger ears to someone else. This might have been with a student, colleague or anyone else in your life. What Judger questions were you listening with? What might you have been assuming about that individual? Looking back, what Learner questions could you have instead listened with? Now, replay the scene. Imagine that this time you are listening with Learner ears. How might that have changed the feeling tone and outcome of the situation?

Exercise #5: Listen to *yourself* with Learner ears. I'm sure you're familiar with the expression, "I'm my own worst critic." That's what happens when we listen to ourselves with Judger ears. Apply the same listening principles as in the exercises above. Ask yourself: "In this moment, am I listening to myself with Learner ears or Judger ears? What questions am I asking about myself? How would I feel about myself if I listened to myself in a kinder way? What questions would help me listen to myself with more appreciation, compassion, and forgiveness?" Over time you'll develop the ability to recognize the Judger questions your inner critic asks, and convert them to Learner questions that allow you to listen to, and be with yourself in more generous, positive, and expansive new ways.

USE THE CHOICE MAP AS A GUIDE

Purpose: As with any map, the Choice Map is a visual reference, in this case to quickly and easily observe the questions you're asking, and the mindset from which you are asking them. You'll also recognize the direction your mindset and those questions are likely to lead you. I like to think of the Choice Map as helping us understand the geography of our own minds.

Discussion: Throughout Emma's story, she learned how to use the Choice Map to become increasingly aware of the kinds of questions she was asking—Learner or Judger—and how to apply this knowledge to change her mindset. She becomes more successful and satisfied with herself as a teacher, with her students, and with Carmen and other colleagues. Changes in Emma's students Becky and Brandon also come about with the help of the Choice Map.

Practice #1: Turn to the Choice Map and imagine that you are the figure standing at the juncture of the paths on the left side of the map. Some thought, feeling, or situation has just happened to you. Relate this to a recent situation in your own life. What happened, and what did you think and feel about it? Experiment by asking yourself Judger and then Learner questions;

then compare the experiences and results you get by following each of the two paths.

Practice #2: Use the Choice Map to learn from a Judger hijack you experienced in the past. How might you have handled that same situation if, instead, your Learner mindset had been in charge?

Practice #3: Use the Choice Map to learn from a past situation that *did* work well for you. What Learner questions made the difference? How did your questions help you avoid the Judger pit? Did you ask Switching questions to move to the Learner path? What were they? What did you learn from this situation that could be valuable guidance in the future?

Practice #4: Share the Choice Map with others. You may know that old medical school adage: "See one, do one, teach one, and it's yours." Reinforce your own learning by introducing the Choice Map to colleagues, students, professional learning groups, reading groups, friends, and family members. Sharing your own success stories of intentionally switching from Judger to Learner is an excellent way to get others engaged so they too can benefit from the principles and guidance of the Choice Map.

(Note: You can download a color version of the Choice Map by accessing the free Learner Mindset experience at the end of this book.)

BENEFIT FROM SWITCHING QUESTIONS

Purpose: To develop *natural* and *intentional* ways to facilitate course corrections when you've landed in Judger mindset and want to quickly get back to Learner territory. You've been asking versions of these Switching questions all your life, probably without doing so consciously; you simply couldn't be as successful as you are without having done that! The goal here is to *groove in* and reinforce a skill that's been intuitive and make it intentional so you can *more predictably* and easily get back to Learner when you want to have more positive interactions and results.

Discussion: Switching questions—that's where the action is! They are the cognitive location of personal power, where you take responsibility for where you are from moment to moment, putting your hands on the steering wheel of your own life. Emma learned about Switching questions from Sophie in Chapter 8, "Easy as ABCD." Here's a summary of the process:

A Aware. Ask yourself, *Am I in Judger?* Or, *Is this working?*

B Breathe! Take a slow, deep, relaxed breath, and exhale fully, to calm and center yourself. This also helps you gain perspective.

C **Curiosity**. Get curious and wonder about what would be best for yourself and others. Then ask yourself a Switching question, such as those listed below.

D **Decide**. Ask yourself: "What do I choose to do *now*?"

Exercise #1: The first Switching question is almost always, "Am I in Judger?" If the answer is yes, and you want to get to Learner instead, ask yourself a few of the different Switching questions below. Experiment to find out which ones work best for you.

- Am I in Judger? Is this working?
- Is this what I want to be feeling or doing?
- What would I rather be feeling and doing?
- What assumptions am I making?
- Am I being objective and honest?
- What are the facts?
- What is the other person thinking, feeling, and wanting?
- How *else* can I think about this?
- What's my choice right now?

Exercise #2: Bring to mind a past situation that was difficult but which you were able to convert into a positive, Learner one. Consider what Switching questions you might have asked, even if you weren't aware of it at the time.

Exercise #3: Think of a current stressful situation you would like to transform from a Judger experience to a Learner one. Ask yourself Switching questions from the list, preferably writing down your answers. Combine this with the ABCD Choice Process. Notice changes in your thinking and feeling and any new possibilities that become available as a result.

ASK THE FIVE QUESTIONS

Purpose: The Five Questions bring together the essential lessons of this book. The more often you use these questions the more naturally and fully you'll integrate them into your everyday thinking. These five questions provide more than quick reminders of the lessons in the book. They are also useful to rely on whenever you encounter a special challenge or wish to prepare for the best possible outcomes in specific situations and relationships. Here's a reminder of the questions.

The Five Questions

1. What do I want—for both myself and others?

2. Am I in Learner mindset or Judger mindset right now?

3. Am I *listening* with Learner ears or Judger ears?

4. What assumptions am I making?

5. Who do I choose to be in this moment?

Discussion: Below you'll find helpful explanations for each of the five questions. Ask yourself all five questions in any situation that occurs in your life when you need to make a decision and respond in the best possible way:

1. **What do I want—for both myself and others?**

Goals and intentions are the "true north" of planning and behavior. Failing to clarify what you want automatically puts any one of us on a shaky course. If you can't state what you want, you'll likely get what you don't want! Or, in the words of Lewis Carroll, "If you don't know where you are going, any road will get you there."

2. **Am I in Learner mindset or Judger mindset right now?**

Simply noticing your mindset in a neutral, non-judgmental way, moment by moment, is essential for becoming free to make the most effective choices about what to do next. If you discover you're in Judger mindset, you can choose to switch to Learner instead. Imagine calling someone for directions to get to their home. The first question they're likely to ask is, "Where are you now?"

3. **Am I *listening* with Learner ears or Judger ears?**

By learning to recognize whether you are listening with Learner or Judger ears, you can take greater responsibility for how your listening impacts your communication with others. If you notice you're feeling either defensive or angry, you may be listening with Judger ears.

4. **What assumptions am I making?**

Continually wondering about assumptions is the core discipline of the most effective thinking and problem-solving. Searching for and challenging assumptions is also the best route for *listening to others with Learner ears*. This is particularly important when interacting with students and colleagues, not to mention on the home front!

5. **Who do I choose to be in this moment?**

This is always the crucial question regardless of the circumstances; it places each of us directly in the present moment as author of our own lives.

CREATE BREAKTHROUGHS WITH Q-STORMING®

Purpose: To generate new questions and thinking that will lead to new possibilities and results.

Discussion: Einstein once said that insanity consists of doing the same thing over and over and expecting different results. That would be like asking the same questions over and over and expecting different answers. If you want a change, an innovation or a breakthrough, only a new question can open that door. Emma and Carmen had an important breakthrough by using a form of Q-Storming during their meeting on the playground as they searched for alternatives to the Behavior Chart. Later in the story they Q-Storm to come up with new ideas to encourage their students to participate more fully in the Open House.

While Q-Storming may resemble brainstorming, the goals of these two practices are significantly different. The goal of brainstorming is to come up with answers and solutions, and this often works. When it doesn't, it's probably because people were looking for answers to the *wrong questions!* By contrast, the goal of Q-Storming is to generate new questions, making it possible to discover fresh answers and new directions and possibilities.

After all, how could you get the best answers from the wrong questions? If you want to do both practices, I suggest starting with Q-Storming. It will improve your chances for successful brainstorming exponentially.

Q-Storming is based on the following premises:

- Great results *begin* with great questions.

- Most problems can be solved with enough of the right *questions.*

- The questions we ask *ourselves* provide the most fruitful openings for new thinking and change. Therefore, in this exercise, all the questions "stormed" are in first person singular or plural (I/we).

- The solutions, answers, and possibilities we seek are often behind closed doors in our minds; the keys you need to open those doors are fresh new questions.

Q-Storming is ideally done with two or more people—the more minds the better—though you can certainly benefit by doing it by yourself. Q-Storming is an ideal practice for cultivating your Inquiring mindset. It's also a great tool for professional learning communities to build more collaborative Learner relationships, and enhance productive conversations, including collaborating on developing curriculum.

The Process: Establish the goal for Q-Storming. For example, Carmen and Emma established the goal of seeking alternatives to the Behavior Chart. Then generate and write down as many questions as fast as you can. Remember that this is a focused time for questions, *not* answers. Avoid any temptations to discuss the questions, provide answers or argue for or against them. After writing down all those questions, review them and see if anything you've already written suggests even more questions.

After this, reflect on the questions for any new ideas, possibilities, and action steps they suggest to you. From all those new questions, it will become evident which ones might lead you to the fresh ideas and solutions you're seeking.

You'll find a whole chapter on Q-Storming® in *Change Your Questions, Change Your Life: 10 Powerful Tools for Life and Work* (second edition).

COLLABORATE WITH PROFESSIONAL LEARNING COMMUNITIES

This tool brings together the Learner mindset tools for fostering collaborative relationships in professional learning communities. While writing *Teaching that Changes Lives*, I frequently turned to Jim Roussin, co-author of *Guiding Professional Learning Communities*.[24] I am greatly indebted to him for his wisdom, generosity, and constructive recommendations throughout the process. Thank you Jim!

In this book, I've tried to provide a picture of how the growth and development of individual teachers, students, administrators, and the culture of the school itself, follow interweaving paths, in this case guided by the Learner Mindset System of Tools and Practices. One of my goals in writing this book was to contribute to the advancement of professional learning communities (PLC) in schools and universities. In my work over many years with groups, these tools have enriched mutual learning and productive, satisfying collaboration, not only for the group itself but for the individuals participating in these groups.

PLC as Team: The success of a PLC, like the success of any team or group endeavor, is characterized by the relationships of its members and the output of their collective efforts. The Learner Mindset System of Tools and Practices, which is at the heart of *Teaching that Changes Lives,* has grown out of similar work I've been doing with teams in organizations for many years. A brief summary of that work is described in "Shifting Mindsets: Questions that Lead to Results," published in the *Wharton Business School Newsletter*[25] (you can download a free copy from my website: www.InquiryInstitute.com).

The more that members of a PLC can function as a learning team, the more successful and satisfied everyone can be—with themselves, each other, and the quality and impact of their work. Given the demanding climate in education today, a well-run PLC offers teachers the refuge and intellectual stimulation of a Learner climate, a "safe container" where members can collaborate and inquire about their work while experiencing acceptance, appreciation, and mutual understanding and respect.

Dedicated to these ends, here's the basic protocol I follow whether working with a team or a PLC: I begin by teaching the basic distinctions of Learner and Judger mindsets, emphasizing the importance of each person developing skills for managing their *own* mindsets. Next, I point out that the Choice Map can be used as a guide for teams as well as for individuals. I often introduce this notion by simply asking, "Has anyone here ever been on a Judger team?" People invariably laugh, intuitively understanding the significance of the term, having suffered adverse experiences as members of such teams.

What I call Learner teams and Judger teams are aligned with descriptions in the literature of *high performing* and *low performing* teams. Low performing teams are characterized by negative emotions and high advocacy with little inquiry. By contrast, high performing teams are characterized by positive emotions, a spirit of collaboration, and a good balance between advocacy and inquiry.[26] I also share practices such as Q-Storming with teams; this provides a creative Learner structure so a team can more efficiently and creatively collaborate on issues, topics, and curriculum under consideration.

Imagine this! Imagine for a moment that everyone in your PLC has read *Teaching that Changes Lives,* and has become skillful with the tools in the workbook. As a team you have also discussed the story and each tool as you might if you were following the discussion guide in a book club, sometimes *applying* a tool to some issue commonly under consideration. Each person in your PLC has grown their inquiring mindset and has developed a resilient Learner mindset. Everyone has made a practice of staying curious, questioning assumptions, and listening to each other with Learner ears. You use the Choice Map as a guide to observe where you are at any moment and you're all adept at asking Switching questions when appropriate. Then one day, in discussing the The Five Questions, one of your colleagues comes up with a different way to ask the last question, "Who do I choose to be in this moment?" He or she suggests that as a team you could be asking *together:* "Who do *we* choose to be in this moment?" Imagine the impact of that new question!

This scenario is not a pipedream. Staff members at a school in Englewood, New Jersey learned about the Learner and Judger mindset distinctions, as well as Q-Storming, through attending my workshop, *Teaching and Thriving in Difficult Times.* Several months later, during a two-day meeting to design curriculum on a particular subject, the faculty found themselves at loggerheads. A few of the teachers were tenaciously advocating for their own positions and not listening generously to one another. After a day and a half, Supervisor of Professional Development and Curriculum Rosemary Seitel, stopped the meeting and suggested they use Q-Storming to move forward together. The result was that, in a single afternoon, the team transitioned from negativity to open-minded neutrality and came to a comfortable, evidence-based consensus on that curriculum.[27]

I am always delighted to hear stories like that one, confirming once again the promise of how these tools can bring people together while revealing a productive path forward, beyond the hurdles that inevitably arise in the process of achieving anything truly worthwhile. Such stories reinforce our awareness of how Learner mindset tools contribute to mutual trust and help to build professional learning communities. Peter Senge speaks of what we can accomplish by "involving everyone in the system in expressing their aspirations, building their awareness, and developing their capabilities together. In a school that learns, people . . . recognize their common stake in the future of the school system and the things they can learn from one another."[28]

I am convinced that professional learning communities can provide the vital pulse for schools that can prepare, in Eric Hoffer's words, "learners who inherit the future." High-performing PLC fortify the capacity for thinking and inquiry, for discernment and innovation, and for clear communication and collaboration. These are essential for making the difference we all so deeply desire for our students and our schools. PLC can be a powerful vehicle for teaching that changes lives. It is my sincere hope that the Learner mindset tools I've described in these pages might contribute to realizing those possibilities.

LEARNER MINDSET ONLINE LEARNING

Visit our website to discover additional ways the Learner Mindset skills can help you: www.LearnerMindsetOnline.com. There are three parts, as follows:

1. **The Choice Map**

   a. Watch a short video of the author demonstrating the core principles of the Choice Map.

   b. Download a full-color version of the Choice Map. You can pin it up at school or at home as a reminder that you can choose between Learner and Judger mindsets.

   c. FAQ's and suggestions for sharing the Choice Map with others.

2. **Interviews**

   Listen to interviews with teachers and educational leaders describing how they have employed this mindset material in many ways, including in the classroom and with professional learning communities.

3. **Learning and Reflection Exercise**

   This practical format of questions guides you in applying the Learner Mindset concepts in your own life, both professionally and personally.

NOTES

1. Schank, Roger. *Teaching Minds: How Cognitive Science Can Save Our Schools.* Teachers College Press, New York & London. 2011.
2. Costa, Art L. and Bena Kallick (Eds.). *Learning and Leading with Habits of Mind: 16 Essential Characteristics for Success.* ASCD Publishers, Alexandria, VA. 2008.
3. Dweck, Carol S. *Mindset: The New Psychology of Success.* Random House, New York, NY. 2006.
4. Dweck, Carol S. "Mindsets and Human Nature: Promoting Change in the Middle East, the Schoolyard, the Racial Divide, and Willpower." *American Psychologist.* November 2012, Vol. 67, No. 8.
5. Goldberg, Marilee C. *The Art of the Question: A Guide to Short-Term Question-Centered Therapy.* John Wiley & Sons, Inc., Hoboken, NJ. 1998.
6. Adams, Marilee. *Change Your Questions, Change Your Life: 10 Powerful Tools for Life and Work* (2nd Ed.). Berrett-Koehler Publishers, San Francisco, CA. 2009.
7. *MetLife Survey of The American Teacher: Teachers, Parents and the Economy.* Report Date: March 2012.
8. *MetLife Survey of The American Teacher: Teachers, Parents and the Economy.* Report Date: March 2012.
9. *MetLife Survey of The American Teacher: Teachers, Parents and the Economy.* Report Date: March 2012.
10. Ginott, Haim G. *Teacher and Child: A Book for Parents and Teachers.* Avon Books, New York, NY. 1972.
11. Marzano, Robert J. "The Inner World of Teaching." *Educational Leadership.* April 2011, Volume 68, Number 7.

12. Hawn, Goldie. *10 Mindful Minutes: Giving Our Children—and Ourselves—the Social and Emotional Skills to Reduce Stress and Anxiety for Healthier, Happier Lives.* A Perigee Book, New York, NY. 2011.
13. Doidge, Norman. *The Brain that Changes Itself: Stories of Personal Triumph from the Frontiers of Brain Science.* Penguin Books, New York, NY. 2007.
14. Frederickson, Barbara L. *Positivity: Groundbreaking Research Reveals How to Embrace the Hidden Strength of Positive Emotions, Overcome Negativity, and Thrive.* Crown Publishers, New York, NY. 2009.
15. Maslow, Abraham H. *Towards a Psychology of Being.* John Wiley & Sons, Inc.,New York, NY. 1998.
16. Tschannen-Moran, Megan and Bob. *Evocative Coaching: Transforming Schools One Conversation at a Time.* Jossey-Bass Publishers, San Francisco, CA. 2010.
17. Goleman, Daniel. *Emotional Intelligence: Why It Can Matter More Than IQ.* Bantam Books, New York, NY. 1995.
18. Barell, John. *Did You Ever Wonder?* International Baccalaureate Organization, 2013.
19. Costa, Arthur L. and Bena Kallick (eds.). *Learning and Leading with Habits of Mind: 16 Essential Characteristics for Success.* ASCD Publishers, Alexandria, VA. 2008.
20. Senge, Peter *et al. Schools That Learn: A Fifth Discipline Fieldbook for Educators, Parents, and Everyone Who Cares About Education.* Nicholas Brealey Publishing, London. 2012. See pages 139-140 for a description of Behavior Over Time (BOT) diagrams.
21. Langer, Ellen J. *The Power of Mindful Learning.* Perseus Books, Cambridge, MA. 1998.
22. Palmer, Parker J. *The Courage to Teach: Exploring the Inner Landscape of a Teacher's Life.* Jossey-Bass Publishers, San Francisco, CA. 2007.
23. Reivich, Karen and Andrew Shatte. *The Resilience Factor: 7 Keys to Finding Your Inner Strength and Overcoming Life's Hurdles.* Broadway Books, New York, NY. 2002.
24. Hord, Shirley M., James L. Roussin and William A. Sommers. *Guiding Professional Learning Communities: Inspiration, Challenge, Surprise, and Meaning.* Corwin Publishers, Thousand Oaks, CA. 2010.
25. "Shifting Mindsets: Questions that Lead to Results." A Nano Tool® for Leaders: *Wharton@Work.* August 2012 Newsletter.
26. Fredrickson, Barbara L. and Marcial F. Losada. "Positive Affect

and the Complex Dynamics of Human Flourishing." *American Psychologist.* October 2005. Vol. 60, No 7.

27. Personal conversation with Rosemary Seitel, M.A., Supervisor of Curriculum and Professional Development, Janis E. Dismus Middle School in Englewood, NJ. March 2013.

28. Senge, Peter et al. *Schools That Learn: A Fifth Discipline Fieldbook For Educators, Parents, And Everyone Who Cares About Education.* Doubleday, New York, NY. 2000.

Notes

ACKNOWLEDGMENTS

In writing this book, I have been enriched, stretched, humbled, and inspired by those who hold teaching and education as a sacred trust. I am deeply grateful to those who have shared and supported this odyssey. They include:

My special thanks to Hal Zina Bennett, author, editor, and writing coach extraordinaire, who brought his wealth of experience, both as a teacher and wordsmith, to this book. His passion for education, questions, and the Learner mindset helped to make the writing of this book a rewarding experience in itself.

My home team makes it all possible. My deepest gratitude to Kim Aubry, Executive Director of the Inquiry Institute, who is key to all our endeavors. My heartfelt thanks also goes to: Robert Burger, Denise Easton, Marina Sinclair, Terry Andrews, Susan Critelli, and Jim Roussin. And enduring appreciation for Ed Adams, my husband, and best friend—the teacher with whom I happily share my life.

Doctors Art Costa and Bena Kallick contributed much more than the Foreword to this book. I am grateful for their friendship, generosity, brilliance, and generative contributions to education throughout the world.

Two organizations have been especially important in supporting the journey of this book: The International Baccalaureate, and Learning Forward New Jersey.

This is my second book with Berrett-Koehler Publishers and I am extraordinarily grateful for their partnership. The BK mission is to contribute to "creating a world that works for all." Their belief that *Teaching that Changes Lives* can make that kind of difference has made all the difference for me. In particular, I thank: Maria Jesús-Aguiló, Charlotte Ashlock, Michael Crowley, Kristen Frantz, David Marshall, Irene Morris, Detta Penna, Steve Piersanti, Dianne Platner, Katie Sheehan, Jeevan Sivasubramaniam, and Rick Wilson.

In multiple and invaluable ways, each of these individuals has also made a notable difference for me and this book: Claire Akselrad, Rebecca Akselrad, Mark Albion, Curtis Aubry, Rachel Aubry, John Barell, Craig Barton, Ilene Becker, Larry Becker, Schon Beechler, Anna Barrett, Dan Blank, Patrick Blessinger, Peter Block, Mrim Boutla, Tara Brach, Alan Briskin, Kathy Browne, Dixon Butler, Judith Cárdenas, Anne Catena, Michael Cohan, Ira Cohen, Karen Collias, Jason Connell, Emma Lasden Crockin, David Dell, Scott DiGiammarino, Mark Dolan, Ellie Drago-Severson, Naomi Drew, Victoria Duff, Jenny Edwards, Dara Elovitch, Jim Evers, Christina Dunn Finegold, Verna Fitzsimmons, Yvonne Gaines, Joanie Geller, Leroy and Selma Goldberg, Pat Goldring, Carmella Granado, Anita and Walter Grazer, Robert Hall, Vicki Halsey, Kevin Hao, Rita J. Hartman, Greg Higgins, Sam Horn, Heidi Hayes Jacobs, Joellen Killion, Marlyn Kline, Kanu Kogod, Robert Kramer, Jeff Kulick, Delmy Lendof, Stewart Levine, Kevin Lohela, Camilla Lopez, Victoria Marsick, John McAuley, Caroline Adams Miller, New Jersey Educational Association, Leydi Ortiz, Bill Osman, Ellyn Phillips, Brad Pressman, Don Proffit, Gemma Qin, Audrey Reed, Warren and Ruth Reed, Kenneth Rhee, Cynda

Rushton, Marge Schiller, Bob Schwartz, Rosemary Seitel, Michele Shay, Kate Sikerbol, Harvey Silver, Melinda Sinclair, Edlyn Smith, Nancy Starmer, Jackie Stavros, Greg Stebbins, Jesse Stoner, Lee Salmon, Choon Seng Ng, Kathy Telban, Robert Tobias, Henry Toi, Carla Van Dyk, Jayan Warrier, Jeff Wetzler, Penny Whitney, Caleb Winebrenner, Jerry Woehr, Ruth Zaplin, Don Zauderer, and Diane Zimmerman.

ABOUT
THE
AUTHOR

Teaching that Changes Lives is Dr. Marilee Adams's third book, expanding her innovative and practical work on questioning, mindsets, and thinking into the world of education. Her first book, *The Art of the Question,* is a behavioral-cognitive textbook which one eminent reviewer described as "a seminal and break-through contribution to the field of psychotherapy." Her second book, *Change Your Questions, Change Your Life,* applies the principles she has been developing over the past 25 years to coaching, business, and the challenges of organizations and change. It is an international bestseller, published in more than 16 languages. Though Marilee herself was never a K–12 teacher like the characters in this book, *Teaching that Changes Lives* was inspired by her lifetime love of learning and her deep respect for the vital role that educators play in all of our lives.

Marilee is the leading expert on Question Thinking™. A dedicated educator, coach, workshop facilitator and keynote speaker, she is an adjunct professor at American University, School of Public Affairs, teaching in the Key Executive Leadership Program. She has also been a guest lecturer at Teachers College at Columbia University and teaches the Learner Mindset System in a wide variety of organizational, educational, and public settings. Her workshops on *Teaching and Thriving in Difficult Times* and *The Learner Mindset Advantage,* as well as the conference she hosted on *Education and the Inquiring Mindset,* have attracted educators from throughout the United States as well as from Canada, mainland China and Singapore.

Dr. Adams has presented her work at Harvard University; Kansas State University; Kent State University; New York University; Northern Kentucky University; Princeton University; Humber University; George Mason University; Georgetown McDonough School of Business, and has consulted for a statewide coaching program of K-12 principals in the state of Texas. She is also an advisor to Learning Forward New Jersey.

She has presented at conferences such as: New Jersey Educational Association; Learning Forward Annual Conference; the International Coach Federation; Pegasus Systems Thinking Conference; Organizational Development Network; Society for Human Resource Management; National Training Laboratory; American Society of Training & Development; Positive Leadership at American University in the Key Executive Leadership Program; and she has been affiliated with Columbia University's Global Learning & Leadership Group at Teachers College.

Her consulting with leading organizations and agencies has provided her with a unique understanding of skills and abilities such as critical thinking, problem-solving, collaboration, innovation, and initiative that students will need for the future. Client organizations include: Ameriprise, Lockheed Martin; Johnson & Johnson; Merck & Co.; Booz Allen; DHL; Brother International; the United States Navy; NASA Goddard; National Defense University; United States Departments of Treasury, Interior, and Education; National Geospatial Agency; Brookings Institution; Johns Hopkins; Toronto General Hospital; Hamilton Health Sciences; and Christiana Care Hospital.

She holds a PhD in Clinical Psychology from the Fielding Graduate University and an MSW from the School of Social Work at Virginia Commonwealth University.

Marilee and her husband, artist and psychologist Ed Adams, live in the river town and arts community of Lambertville, New Jersey.

ABOUT THE INQUIRY INSTITUTE

Dr. Marilee Adams and her colleagues at the Inquiry Institute share a passion for learning and for making a positive difference for K-12 teachers, students and schools, as well as for educators and students in higher learning. We offer unique, innovative tools for creating a climate of learning and improving job satisfaction for teachers and other professionals throughout the educational spectrum. Our work at the Inquiry Institute is informed by the principles, practices, and tools of the Learner Mindset System described in this book. Here's a partial list of the resources you'll discover at our website:

- The Learner Mindset Advantage Workshops and Programs
- Learner Mindset Intensive Program
- "Chief Question Officer" Certificate Program
- Q Storming® Training Programs
- Coaching for Teachers and Educational Leaders
- Membership in Online Learning Community
- Professional Learning Community Resources
- Learner Mindset eLearning Programs for Educators

Marilee Adams, Ph.D. is available for keynote presentations, consulting, coaching, and workshops, both on-site and virtual.

We'd Love to Hear From You: We are eager to receive your success stories, suggestions, and questions. Let's be in touch!

The Inquiry Institute
10 York Street, P.O. Box 339
Lambertville, New Jersey 08530-3204
Phone: 800-250-7823
Email: Info@InquiryInstitute.com
www.InquiryInstitute.com

Also by Marilee Adams, PhD

Change Your Questions, Change Your Life

10 Powerful Tools for Life and Work, Second Edition, Revised and Expanded

Foreword by Marshall Goldsmith

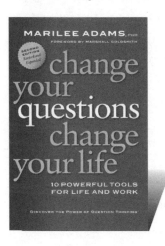

This is the bestselling book that introduced Question Thinking™, the Choice Map™, and the Learner and Judger mindsets to the world. Readers said they personally experienced changing their lives by learning to ask the *right* questions—ones that empower people rather than get in their way. This insight leads the book's hero to breakthroughs that save his career as well as his marriage. In this extensively revised second edition, Adams made her quick-read story even more illuminating and helpful, adding new chapters as well as three powerful new tools. This entertaining, enlightening step-by-step guide has what you need to transform your life, personally and professionally.

Paperback, 216 pages, ISBN 978-1-57675-600-3
PDF ebook, ISBN 978-1-60509-430-4

BK Berrett–Koehler Publishers, Inc.
San Francisco, *www.bkconnection.com*   **800.929.2929**

Praise for *Change Your Questions, Change Your Life*

"The ideas in *Change Your Questions, Change Your Life* have had a profound impact on me and my business. Few books offer such potential to change *everything* in your work and life. Read this book and learn how to use the power of Question Thinking to revolutionize your thinking, solutions, and results."
— Larina Kase, PsyD, MBA, author of *The Confident Leader* and coauthor of the *New York Times* bestseller *The Confident Speaker*

"Transformation, for individuals or organizations, always begins with new questions. Marilee Adams gives us simple yet incredibly powerful tools for finding our way to questions that change our lives."
— Myron Rogers, coauthor of *A Simpler Way*

"In Congress or the physics lab, I focus on the important skill of asking myself the tough questions, framed in a way that they can be answered constructively. Marilee Adams's enlightening book teaches, in a skillful, readable way, techniques for asking the right questions so we can achieve preferred outcomes in our personal and professional lives—and also in how we can contribute as thoughtful citizens."
— Rush Holt, U.S. Congressman

"Marilee Adams's insightful Question Thinking technology provides a precision of thought and inquiry that enables people to quickly get to the core of issues. We urgently need this kind of fresh approach to a 'transpartisan' perspective for dealing with the complex problems of our world. I strongly recommend her unique and powerful work."
— Don Edward Beck, PhD, coauthor of *Spiral Dynamics*

"Well done, Dr. Adams. *Change Your Questions, Change Your Life* is the rare book that I use almost every day. I asked Learner questions to quickly transform a delicate organizational situation that had seemed intractable for a whole year. Your Question Thinking work changes paradigms, organizations, and lives. It's a classic!"
— Rev. Dr. John McAuley, President and CEO, Muskoka Woods

"I really did love this book—and it's one of the most practical I've ever read. The greatest thing is that it's not a 'one and done' kind of book. You'll find yourself going back to it again and again. And you'll definitely find yourself sharing it with friends and colleagues. I know I have."
— Tracy Davidson, Anchor and Consumer Reporter, NBC 10 News Philadelphia

"Question Thinking offers patients, families, and clinicians a new paradigm for patient and relationship centered care. The simple yet profound framework of questions has the potential to contribute, at every level, to the transformation of heath care."
— Cynda Hylton Rushton, PhD, RN, FAAN, Associate Professor, Nursing and Pediatrics, Johns Hopkins University School of Nursing, Robert Wood Johnson Executive Nurse Fellow

"We've used Question Thinking so successfully in our simulations that it led to a radical transformation in how people approach problems. It also made an immediate and sustained change in their behavior. In an organizational culture, the more people can be taught these processes, the greater positive impact it can have on productivity and the bottom line."
— Carmella Granado, Senior Director of Organizational Effectiveness, Flextronics

"Marilee is smarter than anyone I know about asking the questions that really matter."
— Lillian Brown, author of *Your Public Best* and *The Polished Politician*, named "one of the 100 most influential PR people of the century" by *PR Week*

"This book is great. I couldn't put it down! It clearly communicates how the questions we ask ourselves and others determine our results—and this makes all the difference for successful sales. I strongly recommend *Change Your Questions, Change Your Life* to everyone who takes my sales courses."
— Jacques Werth, coauthor of *High Probability Selling*

"This book is an invitation to success for individuals and organizations. Dr. Marilee Adams has created a surprisingly simple and powerful practice for learning that propels us to our goals. Best of all, the same practices that make a difference for individuals also offer practical and impactful guidelines for learning organizations."
— Victoria J. Marsick, PhD, Professor, Teachers College, Columbia University, and coauthor of *Sculpting the Learning Organization*

"A breath of fresh air. Of course, both questions and answers are necessary, but if you only focus on answers, the world becomes a very small place indeed. Marilee Adams helps open the door to innovation, creativity, and inspiration. This book is a treasure chest."
— Harrison Owen, founder of Open Space Technology and author of *Wave Rider*

"This book may cause organizational leaders to take another look at their lists of competencies. If Question Thinking isn't already there, it may be time to go back to the drawing board. Marilee demonstrates why this capacity is absolutely essential to organizational and leadership success—and how easily it can be acquired."
—Beverly Kaye, PhD, coauthor of *Love 'Em or Lose 'Em* and *Love It, Don't Leave It*

"It was through the use of Dr. Adams's Question Thinking tools that I was able to help people reach a meaningful and successful resolution for a highly controversial project. Shifting from a Judger mentality to a solution-oriented one helped people move out of adversarial roles and enabled them to co-create a shared community."
—Tracey Pilkerton Cairnie, MS, Adjunct Professor, Conflict Analysis and Resolution, George Mason University

"Marilee's Question Thinking work shows us how to use questions to illuminate choices and help us understand how to manage our work and private lives in the most positive and productive ways. Marilee is a terrific presenter, and her workshops for our high-potential leaders made a significant and positive impact."
—Liz Barron, Director, Executive Leadership Programs, The Brookings Institution

"This fable is destined to be a classic in the Og Mandino genre. Question Thinking will make your life more effective regardless of personal history, personality type, or profession. Buy this book and read it tonight. Your life will never be the same."
—Stewart Levine, author of *The Book of Agreement* and *Getting to Resolution*

"*Change Your Questions, Change Your Life* is an amazing conversation. With clarity and accessibility, Marilee models a process whereby we can intentionally change our way of internal inquiry. Imagine being in conscious charge of our own thoughts! A wonderful tool for coaches, helping professionals, and all who desire to transform their inner conversations."
—Pamela Richarde, Master Certified Coach, Past President, International Coach Federation

"Question Thinking is brilliant and simple. Marilee demonstrates how you can use the power of questions to transform any and every area of your life. By changing your questions you are able to transform the way you think, the way you act, and importantly, the results you can achieve. This book is an ideal guide for anyone looking for positive results at work or at home."
—Lori Sheppard, President, EDGEucation Worldwide Enterprises

"I read this book cover to cover *twice*. I had valuable insights each time! I also think it would be exceedingly smart for politicians and diplomats to use Dr. Adams's questioning methodologies. It could make our world a safer place."
   —David Pensak, PhD, author of *Innovation for Underdogs*

"This is a must-read for any leader who wants to produce powerful results. The tools presented are straightforward yet extremely effective in helping the reader learn to ask empowering questions—those that inspire, motivate, and produce positive change. This book demonstrates that Question Thinking can truly change your personal and professional life."
   —Tara Gomez, Manager of Employee Development, Strategic Learning
      Services, United States Postal Inspection Service and Office of the
      Inspector General

"Question Thinking is groundbreaking work, and Dr. Marilee Adams is the thought leader who introduced it to the world. I find *Change Your Questions, Change Your Life* inspired and transformational. So do my students of Action Learning. They consistently find that these question methodologies help them unleash and fulfill the true potential of Action Learning."
   —John Czajkowski, School of Public Affairs, American University

"Questions, more than answers, have the power to change our lives. Question Thinking brings you into a world of successful problem solving and decision making. This book delivers the goods: transformation, improved judgment, and innovation. Can a book really change your life? The answer is 'Yes!'"
   —Hildy and Stan Richelson, authors of *Bonds: The Unbeaten Path to
      Secure Investment Growth*

"Using Question Thinking skills has transformed how I see and operate in the world. I'm far more effective as a coach and as a manager. My marriage is stronger and more enjoyable, and I also believe I'm a better parent. My daughter even loves sharing the Choice Map with her friends and teachers!"
   —Kim Aubry, Life Coach

Berrett–Koehler
Publishers

A community dedicated to creating
a world that works for all

Visit Our Website: www.bkconnection.com

Read book excerpts, see author videos and Internet movies, read
our authors' blogs, join discussion groups, download book apps, find
out about the BK Affiliate Network, browse subject-area libraries of
books, get special discounts, and more!

Subscribe to Our Free E-Newsletter, the BK *Communiqué*

Be the first to hear about new publications, special discount offers,
exclusive articles, news about bestsellers, and more! Get on the list
for our free e-newsletter by going to www.bkconnection.com.

Get Quantity Discounts

Berrett-Koehler books are available at quantity discounts for orders
of ten or more copies. Please call us toll-free at (800) 929-2929 or
email us at bkp.orders@aidcvt.com.

Join the BK Community

BKcommunity.com is a virtual meeting place where people from
around the world can engage with kindred spirits to create a world
that works for all. BKcommunity.com members may create their own
profiles, blog, start and participate in forums and discussion groups,
post photos and videos, answer surveys, announce and register for
upcoming events, and chat with others online in real time. Please join
the conversation!

BK Berrett–Koehler
Publishers

Berrett-Koehler is an independent publisher dedicated to an ambitious mission: *Creating a World That Works for All.*

We believe that to truly create a better world, action is needed at all levels—individual, organizational, and societal. At the individual level, our publications help people align their lives with their values and with their aspirations for a better world. At the organizational level, our publications promote progressive leadership and management practices, socially responsible approaches to business, and humane and effective organizations. At the societal level, our publications advance social and economic justice, shared prosperity, sustainability, and new solutions to national and global issues.

A major theme of our publications is "Opening Up New Space." Berrett-Koehler titles challenge conventional thinking, introduce new ideas, and foster positive change. Their common quest is changing the underlying beliefs, mindsets, institutions, and structures that keep generating the same cycles of problems, no matter who our leaders are or what improvement programs we adopt.

We strive to practice what we preach—to operate our publishing company in line with the ideas in our books. At the core of our approach is stewardship, which we define as a deep sense of responsibility to administer the company for the benefit of all of our "stakeholder" groups: authors, customers, employees, investors, service providers, and the communities and environment around us.

We are grateful to the thousands of readers, authors, and other friends of the company who consider themselves to be part of the "BK Community." We hope that you, too, will join us in our mission.

A BK Life Book

This book is part of our BK Life series. BK Life books change people's lives. They help individuals improve their lives in ways that are beneficial for the families, organizations, communities, nations, and world in which they live and work. To find out more, visit www.bk-life.com.